Know
WHY
You
Believe

"Shortly after my conversion in 1968, I was given a copy of *Know Why You Believe* and it was what sparked my own lifelong interest in Christian apologetics. Through the years its quality has been demonstrated by its longevity. Now in this updated and expanded version, Paul Little's book can continue to provide hope and help to a new generation of truth-seekers."

J.P. Moreland, Professor of Philosophy
Talbot School of Theology, Biola University
author of *Scaling the Secular City: A Defense of Christianity*

Know WHY You Believe

PAUL E. LITTLE

Updated and Expanded by Marie Little

Cook Communications

Special thanks to Brad Mitchell,
Director of Men's Ministries,
Willow Creek Community Church

Victor is an imprint of
Cook Communications Ministries, Colorado Springs, Colorado 80918
Cook Communications, Paris, Ontario, Canada
Kingsway Communications, Eastbourne, England

Editors: Jerry Yamamoto and Greg Clouse
Study Questions: Afton Rorvik
Cover Design: Bill Gray
Interior Design: RJS Design
Cover Photo: Image Bank

© 1967, 1980, 1987, 1999 by Marie Little. All rights reserved.
Printed in the United States of America.

3 4 5 6 7 8 9 10 Printing / Year 03 02 01 00

Library of Congress Cataloging-in-Publication Data

Little, Paul E.
    Know Why You Believe / by Paul Little.
      p. cm.
    Originally published: 3rd ed. Downers Grove, Ill. : InterVarsity Press, 1988.
      ISBN 1-56476-754-X
      1. Apologetics. I. Title.
    [BT1102.L5 1999]
    239-dc21   98-53688
                                      CIP

Contents

How This Book Began

"After 2,000 Years, No Question Is Going To Bring Christianity Crashing."

With cryptic statements like this, my husband, Paul, found his niche in university settings talking to students about Christianity.

Paul's first assignment as a new staff member with InterVarsity Christian Fellowship was to lead a dinner discussion at the University of Kansas. Fearfully he approached the designated "Greek" house for a 6 P.M. dinner where he would give a fifteen-minute introductory talk followed by questions from the men. His fears were magnified because it was a scholarship hall—really brainy students. Further, it was a Jewish scholarship hall! He later described his prayer that day as he walked to the door of the fraternity house:

"Lord, you know I always stub my toe when I try to explain Christian basics clearly to people with questions. Why must I begin in a residence reserved for the smartest students? They'll tear me apart limb from limb. I'll not live the night out!"

To his amazement, one young man had his life turned around that night by the new thought that God offered him a brand-new life and power to live it. He decided to become a Christian

Encouraged by the good response from this one man, Paul continued. He traveled from campus to campus, leading dorm and fraternity sessions and tirelessly spending hours talking one-on-one with students. From hundreds of campuses on five continents he sought to capture the attention of the bored, the intellectual, the athletic. He used clipped questions to jog the thinking and help the listeners examine their present worldviews, ranging from scientific determinism to placid relativism. He sprinkled in a few "sure-fire" jokes and other good humor. He'd even say, "You exercised blind faith if you ate in a restaurant today." "Believing something doesn't make it true; refusing to believe it doesn't make it false." "Many people who say they don't believe the Bible have actually never read it."

In twenty-five years of lecturing, Paul discovered that regardless of the group there were twelve commonly asked questions. "They are predictable," he said. "If we think through the answers to the common questions we hear, we'll know the answers to the right ones. Right answers to the wrong questions aren't of much help!" From his own study of the Bible and research of biblical scholars, he framed his answers. That's how *Know Why You Believe* was born.

The message of this newly edited book is entirely Paul's. I have added some exciting new illustrations from the specialized fields of archaeology and science. In each area, I have followed the capsulized biblical basics, which are Paul's intentional focus. The Bible has been shown to be stalwart and trustworthy in the light of any challenge. As Paul said, "No one will think up a question that will bring Christianity crashing even after 2,000 years."

It has been twenty-four years since the day when the dread news came of Paul's death in an automobile accident. I am awed that God has continued to use these answers. Paul would say, "These are God's thoughts; the light comes from Him." The many stories I continue to hear of God using these words affirm the extraordinary impact of God's truth, which we all seek.

Just recently I gave a copy of this book to a searching young Sikh woman. After she and her husband visited with me several times in my living room she told me, "This book answered all my questions." She became a fully devoted follower of Jesus Christ—additionally, a sterling wife and mother. Amazing grace.

Marie Little
Mt. Prospect, Illinois

Is Christianity Rational?

W hat is faith?" asked the Sunday School teacher. A young boy answered in a flash, "Believing something you know isn't true."

Actually it's not surprising that many people who investigate faith and Christianity define it this way. In reality, many Christians overtly or secretly also hold this view. For twenty-five years I've been asking this question in college and university bull sessions across the country. The average student of higher education might give the same answer as the boy. It may be couched in different terms, but the idea of self-deception and unreliability is usually associated with the Christian faith.

In these sessions I describe in simple terms the definition of faith given in the Bible, then ask for questions. The responses are eye-opening.

Don't Kiss Your Brains Good-Bye

First-time investigators will quizzically remark that the sessions have been helpful because they have heard a down-to-earth, concise summation of the Christian message for the first time. At times even committed Christians admit they are relieved to hear the Christian story coherently defended in the open marketplace of ideas. They see they haven't kissed their brains good-bye in becoming Christians!

We live in an increasingly sophisticated and educated world where new choices purloin our attention. Unknowingly, our certainties become diluted with attractive indulgences and our belief systems wobble. This kind of world heightens our need to know why we believe and what are the truths that support that belief. What truths do we live by?

On the important question of whether Christianity is rational and can withstand scrutiny, we begin with the widely misunderstood word *faith*. Aside from religious faith of any genre, we all use faith every day.

• In multiple ways we live by faith, by what we do, what we eat, and whom we trust. We have faith in the doctor, faith in the grocery store, faith in the person who asks us for a date. Even faith that the train will arrive to take us to work, or the mail carrier will bring our paycheck. The scientist has faith in the scientific method learned from previous scientists, assuming they were honest. In every instance, the object of our faith may or may not prove trustworthy. A sad example of misplaced faith came to me recently when a young student discovered his girlfriend had long been going out with another man and would soon marry him. Any relationship is unavoidably built on some degree of faith in the other.

• In each instance, our faith is only as valid as the object in which it is placed. Trust an untested food, an unqualified doctor, or a dishonest person, and the faith is not valid. Usually we assume the reliability of the person or thing in each instance. The faith may be well intentioned, but the object unproven.

• Whatever the objects of our faith, it is commendable to check their reliability, be willing to investigate, and know the truth. If a clock is wrong, we adjust it. It's the sensible thing to do.[1]

Examine Our Prior Thinking

These few examples of faith help us see faith as a normal part of our lives. From there we turn to examine as objectively as possible the rationality of the Christian faith. Objectivity is inevitably colored by our *prior* thinking about Christianity. What facts do we know about it? Do we view it as rational or irrational? Relevant or irrelevant? In those student bull sessions, their prior thinking was glaringly obvious in the questions they asked. Some questions had to do mostly with a lack of information, others with a misunderstanding of the basic content of Christianity Others had penetrating questions, "why" enigmas declared with deep earnestness.

One's prior thinking is a key factor. "What you think you know can hurt you" was the title of an article in the *Chicago Tribune.* "A little knowledge can turn out to be harmful to your financial health" was the subtitle. This article listed fifteen or more examples of befuddled thinking common to investors, like "I try to save money by going to the store every time there's a sale." Too little knowledge of what the Christian faith is all about might also be harmful. In what areas have we been crystal clear about true Christianity and where have we been befuddled in our thinking?

In addition to our prior thinking, another cloud to faith is our "emotional quotient," or E.Q., as it is now called. Whether our heritage is the United States or some other country, there may have been both erroneous and obnoxious examples of practicing Christians who have turned us off. Our E.Q. may hit the sky when Christians are even mentioned. Granted, we all have emotional hang-ups of some kind, but awareness of them does help. On the other hand, we may have had zero contacts with Christians or Christianity; thus no information, no hang-ups. In either case, the more we can comprehend our own origins of thinking and feeling, the more objectively we will be able to consider "the case for Christianity," as C.S. Lewis put it.

Biblical Christianity is anchored on a specific, understandable base. It's not an esoteric religion. According to Christian scholar R.C. Sproul, its content is not concealed in vague symbols. When someone tells you in a hushed whisper that the meaning to life is "one hand clapping" as the Zen Buddhists do, that's esoteric, Sproul states. This is not what we know as a rational basis for thinking. Certainly it is not the idea we intend to convey by "rational thinking."[2]

Meanwhile, the onslaught of diverse views against the Christian faith continues to grow. From the nineteenth century, Western philosophers such as Friedrich Neitzsche have asserted the death of God. Julian Huxley's *Religion without Revelation* is a good example of a popular book that supports this view that God is dead. And we even hear this statement within some quarters in Christendom! Moreover, ethical humanism is having stronger appeal within our society. While Western philosophy is attacking the Christian faith in most university classrooms, any number of Eastern religions have claimed spiritual experiences identical to the Christian faith. Since religious pluralism has dominated the communication media within our global society, we are likely to hear that

> **No opinion poll is going to make God go away.**

- all religions are equally valid,
- contradictions between religious systems are fully acceptable,
- and absolute truth does not exist.

Christianity Tested Objectively?

The analytical philosopher Antony Flew states that to the person who is searching, religious assertions *incapable of being tested objectively* are meaningless. He illustrates this point from a graphic tale told by John Wisdom:

> Once upon a time two explorers came upon a clearing in the jungle. In the clearing were growing many flowers and many weeds. One explorer says, "Some gardener must tend this plot." The other disagrees, "There is no gardener." So they pitch their tents and set a watch. No gardener is ever seen. "But perhaps he is an invisible gardener." So they set up a barbed wire fence. They electrify it. They patrol with bloodhounds. (For they remember how H.G. Wells' *The Invisible Man* could be both smelled and touched though he could not be seen.) But no shrieks ever suggest that some intruder has received a shock. No movements of the wire ever betray an invisible climber. The bloodhounds never give cry. Yet still the believer is not convinced. "But there is a gardener, invisible, insensible to electric shocks, a gardener who comes secretly to look after the garden which he loves." At last the skeptic despairs, "But what remains of your original assertion? Just how does what you call an invisible, intangible, eternally elusive gardener differ from an imaginary gardener or even from no gardener at all?"[3]

Evangelical scholar John Montgomery comments on this story. "In Christianity we do not have merely an allegation that the garden of this world is tended by a loving Gardener; we have the actual *empirical entrance* of the Gardener into the human scene in the person of Jesus Christ (John 20:14-15), and this entrance is verifiable by way of his resurrection."[4]

A Rational Body of Truth

Too often the Christian faith is not considered seriously, but instead as merely one of a number of truth claims, and it is not seen as built on any verifiable truth. Indeed, faith and superstition look like partners.

However, the opposite is true. The Bible itself stresses the importance of revealed rational processes. Jesus stressed this to His disciples, "Love the Lord your God with all your heart . . . and with all your mind" (Matt. 22:37). The whole person is involved in putting our faith in Him: the mind, the emotions, and the will. The Apostle Paul described himself as "defending and confirming the gospel"; that is, giving an apologetic for his faith (Phil. 1:7). All of this implies a clearly understandable message that can be rationally understood and supported.

An unenlightened mind is one never exposed to the truth of God, but enlightenment brings satisfying comprehension when based on a rational body of truth. Every one of us from childhood on needs reasons and explanations. Tell a child he'll get burned if he touches a hot grill. Only then can he make the choice to touch or not touch. But he has been enlightened. So it is for us; enlightenment comes from knowledge of the primary Christian truths.

The Christian faith is always equated with truth. And truth is

> **Belief doesn't create truth. Unbelief doesn't destroy truth.**
>
> **Christian faith goes BEYOND reason, but not AGAINST reason.**

always the opposite of error (2 Thes. 2:11-12). One who has not yet believed is defined by Paul as one who "reject[s] the truth" (Rom. 2:8). It follows, these statements would be meaningless unless there were a way to establish truth objectively. If there were no such possibility, truth and error would, for all practical purposes, be the same. The root question is, does absolute truth exist? One clear evidence is given us.

Creation Makes It Plain

Creation itself, the Apostle Paul states logically, gives all people enough knowledge to know there is a God. The Bible says, "God has made it plain to them" (Rom. 1:19). God is easy to see; He is not hidden. In fact, Paul told his readers to look at creation. "For since the creation of the world God's invisible qualities . . . have been clearly seen" (v. 20). Indeed, two major qualities of God are equally evident for all to see: *"his eternal power and divine nature"* (v. 20).

From this small, yet potent, verse we see that God expects us to believe in Him based on comprehensible evidence. He gives us intelligent and logical reasons. He is saying, "Look at the natural world, even the universe or your own body, and you will have ample evidence for belief in a Creator." The "handiwork," the uncommon masterpiece of the divine Creator, tells us that this is true. Furthermore, He is constantly involved in His creation, which He cares for meticulously.

His "eternal power" is a phrase not easy to wrap our thinking around. Bill Hybels, pastor of Willow Creek Community Church, gives us a glimpse. "God knows everything. No questions can confound him . . . but this knowledge extends even farther than today's events. God knows how all things work. Think about that. He has all the complete knowledge of all of the mysteries of biology, physiology, zoology, chemistry, psychology, geology, physics, medicine, and genetics. He knows the ordinaces of heaven, as well as the reasons and course for the sun and the moon and the clouds."[5] We could say this gives a definition of "infinite," contrasted with our own finiteness. Furthermore, God knows the big picture of every facet of our personal lives.

Seeing the Big Picture

Our incentive for exploring some answers is the prospect of seeing how our individual lives fit into "the big picture" from God's perspective.

Why are we here, living in this family and this place? Does it matter what choices I make and what I do each day? How did I happen to be in this country, not some other? What will happen when I leave this life?

Volumes have been written on the "why" of our existence; hence it is not a new question. It is something we all ask at some time or other. In his widely selling book, *A Brief History of Time*, Stephen Hawking sums up his lifetime of research and thinking by asking one last question. After concluding his ideas on the "what" and the "how" of the universe, he states (seemingly with longing to know the answer), "Now if we only knew the why, we would have the mind of God."[6] Is his yearning to know truly from his heart, or is it simply a sense of emptiness and loss that provokes his question? One wonders.

Yet for many that longing to know is very real. One long time movie actress aptly described it as a "hole in the soul" that started her seeking. The essence of God's picture for us in the Bible is to give us the answers. We need not stay in the dark. There is every evidence of God wanting us to know the answers.

C.S. Lewis explains, "It is easy to say we believe a rope to be strong and sound as long as we are merely using it to wrap a box. But suppose you had to hang by that rope over a precipice. You would really want to first discover how trustworthy that rope was."[7]

Moral Smoke Screens

The moral issue can be a hindrance for many of us, overshadowing the intellectual revelation of God and darkening our understanding. The moral pull can be intractable, insatiable, unwilling to go away. In some cases, the true issue is not that people cannot believe—it is that they *will* not believe.

Jesus was straightforward when He told the highly religious

> **If morality is only "feeling derived," WHO MAKES THE RULES?**
>
> **If Christianity is only "feeling derived," it leads to absurdity. Faith involves mind and heart.**

Pharisees, the legalistic rulers of His day, that their unwillingness to believe was the root of their problem. "You refuse to come to me," He said to them, "to have life" (John 5:40). Then, Jesus added that when a moral commitment is made, it brings understanding to the mind. It even brings resolution to intellectual roadblocks. "If anyone chooses to do God's will, he will find out whether my teaching comes from God or whether I speak on my own" (John 7:17). Alleged intellectual problems are often a smoke screen, covering moral slippage. "Fail in an instant no man did, slipping is crashes law" was Emily Dickinson's definition.

Another digression I've heard is "If Christianity is rational and true, why is it that most educated people don't believe it?" The answer is simple. They don't believe it for the same reason that most uneducated people don't believe it. They don't *want* to believe it. It's not a matter of brain power, for there are outstanding Christians in every field of the arts and sciences. Belief is ultimately a matter of the will. And God has given us starting evidence with creation.

A student once told me I had satisfactorily answered all his questions. "Are you going to become a Christian?" I asked.

"No," he replied.

Puzzled, I asked, "Why not?"

He admitted, "Frankly, because it would mess up the way I'm living." He realized the real issue for him was not intellectual understanding, but moral conviction.

John Stott struck a balance when he summarized how to explain the Christian story: "We cannot pander to a man's intellectual arrogance, but we must cater to his intellectual integrity."

Doubt Strikes Terror

Even committed Christians question their faith and wonder whether it's true. Doubt can strike terror to the soul and be suppressed in an unhealthy way. Those who have grown up in Christian homes and in the Christian church find it easy to doubt the authenticity of their early experiences. From their youth they have accepted the facts of Christianity solely on the basis of confidence and trust in parents, friends, and pastors. As the educational process develops, there is a reexamination of how much of their early teaching they own for themselves.

Such an experience is healthy and necessary to make virile faith genuine. It's nothing to fear or to be shocked about. At times when I travel to new places, I tend to ask myself, looking at unfamiliar streets and people, "Little, how do you know you haven't been taken in by a colossal propaganda program? After all, you can't see God, touch Him, taste Him, or feel Him." And then I go on to ask myself how I know the Gospel is true. I always come back to two basic factors:

- The objective, external, historical facts of the Resurrection,
- The subjective, internal, personal experience of Jesus Christ that I have known in my own life.

When a person, young or old, begins to question and God seems far away, doubts should be welcomed as a way to grow. A Christian can help by welcoming the honesty and openness, creating a climate in which a person feels free to "unload" and express his or her doubts. If not, a young person can be driven underground and turned away by the adult's high-shock index, implying a good Christian would never doubt. The questioner feels harshly judged and so turns away. Young people aren't stupid. I've seen some who have met an unloving response and quickly shift gears, mouth the party line, even though it doesn't come from the heart. When they are out from under pressure to conform, they shed their faith like a raincoat that has never become their very own.

Doubt and questioning are normal to any thinking person. Rather than express shock, listen to the questioner and, if possible, even sharpen the question further. Then an answer can be suggested. Unflinchingly, we can discuss problems, because Christianity centers on the One who is Truth, and scrutiny is no threat.

Don't Hit the Panic Button

For any of us, if we don't find an answer to a question immediately, we needn't hit the panic button. We can keep searching, crystallize the question, and check out books spe-

DOES THE HUMAN SPIRIT NEED FAITH IN GOD?

Does a car need a driver?

Does a car run on soda water?

Does a tree need roots?

Does your soul feel empty?

cializing on seemingly unsolvable questions. It is improbable that anyone thought up, last week, the question that will bring Christianity crashing down. Brilliant minds have probed through the profound questions of every age and have ably answered them.

Full answers to every possible question may allude us. We are not God! The Lord hasn't fully revealed His mind to us on every conceivable query. "The secret things belong to the Lord our God, but the things revealed belong to us and to our children forever" (Deut. 29:29). This is not a cop-out! In fact, God gives us enough information to have a solid foundation under our faith. Christianity is based on *reasonable* faith.

If the thought of checking out the mountain of evidence overwhelms you, again, don't panic. In the college and university setting the audience may be composed of 98 percent agnostics. After a while, it's usually possible to predict the questions they ask in the course of a half-hour question period. The questions may vary in wording, but the underlying issues are the same. This consistency was a great help to me in knowing the major questions and where to sharpen my own knowledge, and how to shape the thoughts in this book.

A Doubter's Response

Doubters have been known to see where troubling issues lie. After hearing answers to their questions, they know that a decision is the next step. They also know that to make no decision is to decide against the Christian position. But for true seekers, though they continue to doubt in the face of adequate information, they should not give up but keep seeking, for eventually God will reward them. Christianity is not a patent medicine. It claims to give an account of facts—to tell you what the real universe is like. "If Christianity is untrue, then no honest person will want to believe it. However, if it is true, every honest person will want to believe it. . . . Christianity will do you good—a great deal more than you ever expected."[8] Therefore, genuine seeking will be rewarded.

This book is intended to spotlight some answers to the commonly asked questions. You can believe it, for Christianity is rational. Indeed, Jesus' words gives us the encouragement to believe: "I have come that [you] may have life, and have it to the full" (John 10:10).

Is There a God?

Throughout human history there is no more profound question demanding an answer. Is there a God? is the question that challenges every thinking person, and the answer has far-reaching implications for each of us no matter where we are in life.

While we were living in Dallas a salesman for the Great Books of the Western World series convinced us to buy the fifty-four-volume set. In the introductory title *The Great Ideas: A Syntopicon of Great Books of the Western World*, I started with number 29 of the 102 ideas presented: God. Editor Mortimer Adler begins by explaining, "In sheer quantity of references, as well as in variety, this is the largest chapter. The reason is obvious. More consequences for thought and action follow the affirmation or denial of God than from answering any other basic question."

Adler goes on to spell out the practical implications: The whole tenor of human life is affected by whether people regard themselves as supreme beings in the universe or acknowledge a superhuman being whom they conceive of as an object of fear or love, a force to be defied or a Lord to be obeyed. Among those who acknowledge a divinity, it matters greatly whether the divine is represented merely by the concept of God—the object of philosophical speculation—or by the living God whom people worship in all the acts of piety, which comprise the rituals of religion.[1]

God in a Test Tube?

It is obvious we cannot examine God in a test tube or prove Him by the usual scientific methodology. Furthermore, we can say with equal emphasis that it is not possible to prove Napoleon by the scientific method. The reason lies in the nature of history itself, and in the limitations of the scientific method. In order for something to be proved by the scientific method, it must be repeatable. A scientist does not announce a new finding to the world on the basis of a single experiment. With history, its very nature is nonrepeatable. No one can rerun the beginning of the universe or bring Napoleon back or repeat the assassination of Lincoln or the crucifixion of Jesus Christ. *Nevertheless, the fact that these events can't be proved by repetition does not disprove their reality as events.*

There are many real things outside the scope of verification by the scientific method. The scientific method is useful only with measurable, material things. No one has ever seen three feet of love or two pounds of justice, but one would be foolish indeed to deny their reality. To insist that God be proved by the scientific method is like insisting that a telephone be used to measure radioactivity.

"Eternity in Our Hearts"

What evidence is there for God? Anthropological research has indicated there is a universal belief in God among the farthest and most remote primitive peoples today. In the earliest histories and legends of peoples all around the world the original concept was of *one* God, who is the Creator. An original *high* God seems once to have been in their consciousness even in those societies that are today polytheistic. Regardless of other accretions added to this unknown God, the idea persisted.

Moreover, in the last fifty years, theological research has challenged the evolutionary concept of religions' development, which asserts that monotheism—the concept of one God—became the apex of a gradual development that began with polytheistic concepts. Instead, it is increasingly clear that the oldest traditions everywhere acknowledged one supreme God.[2]

No wonder men and women since ancient times have longed to know this supreme God. The writer of Ecclesiastes referred to God as having "set eternity in the hearts of men" (Ecc. 3:11). Blaise Pascal, the great seventeenth-century mathematician, wrote of "the God-shaped vacuum" in every person. Perhaps Augustine, the fifth-century church father, said it best: "Our hearts are restless until they rest in thee."

For our present purposes, the evidence includes the fact that a vast majority of humanity has believed in some kind of god or gods at all times and in all places. Though this fact is not conclusive proof by any means, it is a beginning reference point to keep in mind as we attempt to answer the big question.

The Law of Cause and Effect

To begin with, consider the law of cause and effect. No effect can be produced without a cause. There's a note on your door. Someone put it there. The painting on the wall. Someone created it. We, as human beings, and the universe itself are effects that must have had a cause. We come eventually to an uncaused cause, who is God.

Bertrand Russell, noted skeptic, makes an astounding statement in his book *Why I Am Not a Christian*. He says when he was a child, "God" was given him as the answer to the many questions he raised about existence. In desperation he asked, "Well, who created God?" When no answer was forthcoming, he says, "My entire faith collapsed." Russell failed to receive an answer to his burning question, and unfortunately his experience is common.

God—the Creator and the Beginner—is eternal by definition. Indeed, He is uncreated. He is self-existent. Were God a created being, He would not be a cause, He would be an effect. Therefore, He would not and could not be God.

R.C. Sproul, author and lecturer, explains, "Being eternal, God is not an effect. Since he is not an effect he does not require a cause. He is uncaused. It is important to note the difference between an uncaused, self-existent eternal being and an effect that causes itself through self-creation."[3]

> **The basic question is not whether God EXISTS, but whether God is GOOD!**

Infinite Time Plus Chance?

No one would think a computer could come into being without an intelligent designer. It is unlikely that a monkey in a print shop could set Lincoln's "Gettysburg Address" in type. If we found a copy of it, we would conclude that an intelligent mind was the only possible explanation for the printing. How much more incredible is it to believe that the universe in its infinite complexity could have happened by chance?

The human body, for instance, is an admittedly astounding and complex organism, a continual marvel of organization, design, and efficiency. So impressed was Albert Einstein with this marvel that he concluded, "My religion consists of a humble admiration of the illuminant superior Spirit who reveals himself in the slight details we are able to perceive with our frail and feeble minds. That deeply emotional conviction of the presence of a superior reasoning power, which is revealed in the incomprehensible universe, forms my idea of God."[4] Sadly, however, to our knowledge Einstein never progressed to a belief in a personal God.

There are basically two choices for Christians and non-Christians alike: Did the universe and the human race begin by chance or by purpose and design?

Scientists have long relied on infinite time plus chance to explain the origin of the universe, and thus this view for them avoids the "unacceptable conclusion" of a divine cause. The common presupposition behind "infinite time plus chance" projects that from:

- An ideally prepared primordial soup,
- Frequent jolts of electrical charges, and
- Unlimited period of time—eons and eons,
- Life forms then would evolve.

The difficulties this theory presents, however, are so enormous that today those same scientists are pointing out its weaknesses.

The distinguished astronomer Sir Fred Hoyle has proposed an analogy to illustrate these difficulties. He asks, "How long would it take a blindfolded person to solve a Rubik's Cube?" If the person made one move per second, without resting, he estimates it would take an astonishing 1.35 trillion years! Therefore, he concludes, when you consider the life expectancy of a human being, a blindfolded person could not solve a Rubik's Cube.

Hoyle then explains that it would be equally difficult for the accidental formation of only one of the many chains of amino acids in a living cell in which there are about 200,000 such amino acids. Now if you would compute the time required to get all 200,000 amino acids for one human cell to come together by chance, it would be about 293.5 times the estimated age of the earth (set at the standard 4.6 billion years). The odds against this happening would be infinitesimally small, far greater than a blindfolded person trying to solve a Rubik's Cube!

In another analogy Hoyle bolsters his argument. He likens this belief in chance to a "junkyard mentality" and asks, "What are the chances that a tornado might blow through a junkyard containing all the parts of a 747, accidentally assemble them into a plane, and leave it ready for takeoff?" Hoyle answers, "The possibilities are so small as to be negligible even if a tornado were to blow through enough junkyards to fill the whole universe!"

In his impressive book *The Intelligent Universe*, Hoyle concludes, "As biochemists discover more and more about the awesome complexity of life, it is apparent that its chances of originating by accident are so minute that they can be completely ruled out. Life cannot have arisen by chance."[5]

Order and Design in the Universe

When we speak of design as opposed to chance, we are referring to the observable parts of our world, the smallest of neutrons and protons and the vastness of the galaxies. Who or what gave the original specifications and information that put it all together? This information is what we mean by design. It would be comparable to looking for the master plan that took glass, metal, and phosphorous and formed those materials into a functioning TV. No one would think of suggesting that "natural selection" or self-assembly produced such a product. Indeed, the term "natural selection" would not be an explanation, it would only be a label. It would not tell us how these parts knew enough to form together for a useful end. Someone had the information that programmed those parts into a TV.

In the same way, the physical systems of our universe loudly proclaim that someone programmed the instructions into the individual parts to produce the world we see. Dr. Robert Gange suggests it would be valid to say it was *intentionally* designed. If someone should claim that living structures can be traced to the physical properties of subnuclear particles, we still need to ask:

- How did these particles arise?
- Why does an electron have exactly the electrical charge and mass that it does?
- Why is it that light travels at precisely the speed it does?
- Who or what dialed the value of the gravitational "constant"?[6]

From the myriad examples we could cite of intentional design, consider the remarkable properties of plain water. Dr. L.J. Henderson enumerates some of these properties:

Water has a high specific heat. Therefore, the chemical reactions within the [human] body are kept rather stable. If water had a *low* specific heat we would "boil over" with the least activity. If we raise the temperature of a solution by ten degrees Centigrade we speed up the reaction by two. *Without this particular property of water, life would hardly be possible.*

The ocean is the world's thermostat, as we have learned from El Niño. It takes a large loss of heat for water to pass from liquid to ice, and for water to become steam quite an intake of energy is required. Hence the ocean is a cushion against the heat of the sun and the freezing blast of the winter. Unless the temperatures of the earth's surface were modulated by the ocean and kept within certain limits, life would either be cooked to death or frozen to death.

Water is the universal solvent. It dissolves acids, bases, and salts. Chemically it is relatively inert providing a medium for reactions without [being involved] in them. In the human blood stream water holds in solution the minimum of *sixty-four substances.* . . . Any other solvent would be a pure sludge. Without the particular property of water, life as we know it would be impossible.[7]

The earth itself is evidence of meticulous design. "If it were much smaller, our atmosphere would be impossible (as on Mercury and the moon); if much larger the atmosphere would contain free hydrogen (as on Jupiter and Saturn). Its distance from the sun is very precise—even a small change would make it too hot or too cold. Our moon, probably responsible for the continents and ocean basins, is unique in our solar system and seems to have originated in a way quite different from the other relatively smaller moons. The tilt of the earth's axis insures the seasons."[8]

Equally amazing examples of design can be seen within living things, including humans. There are *approximately 11 million species of life on earth* and each one is a living miracle. They are the result of mind-boggling organizational intricacies at the molecular level that leave us in awe. Consider the human eye. The English theologian William Paley pointed to the "fitting together efficiently and cooperatively of the lens, retina and brain; enabling humans to have vision; as conclusive evidence of the design of an all-wise Creator. Thus the functional design of organisms and their features are taken as evidence of the existence of the Designer."[9]

Even Darwin himself in a chapter titled "Difficulties with the Theory" from his *The Origins of Species* states, "To suppose that the eye, with so many parts all working together . . . could have formed by natural selection, seems, I freely confess, absurd in the highest degree."

Harvard's Richard Lewontin, an evolutionist, states that organisms "appear to have been carefully and artfully designed" and calls the perfection of organisms "the chief evidence of a Supreme Designer."[10]

The Universe Had a Beginning

In addition to design in the universe, there is the implication that the universe had in some sense a beginning—a moment in time that brought the world into being. The Bible describes it this way: "In the beginning you [Lord] laid the foundations of the earth, and the heavens are the work of your hands" (Ps. 102:25).

Scientists avoid the idea that time has a beginning or an end because it suggests divine preexistence and intervention. Through the years a number of alternative theories have been developed.

• One attempt was the *"continuous creation/steady-state" model* of the universe proposed in 1948 by Hermann Bondi, Fred Hoyle, and Tom Gold. Dr. James Brooks describes this model this way: "In the steady-state model, it was proposed that as the galaxies moved farther away from each other, new galaxies were formed in between, out of matter that was being 'continually created.' The universe would therefore look more or less the same at all times and its density would be roughly constant. This projected model suggests matter (in the form of hydrogen) is always being created from nothing, and comes about in order to counteract the dilution of material which occurs as the galaxies drift away from each other."[11] His conclusion from this and other factors is that the universe had no beginning and is eternal.

Dr. Robert Jastrow, founder of NASA's Institute for Space Studies, explains that the opposite is true. The moment a star is born, it begins to *consume* some of the hydrogen in the universe, and there is a continual dilution of both hydrogen and the heavier metals in the universe today. He concludes that the theory of an eternal universe is untenable.[12]

• A second explanation posed by scientists for the beginning of the universe has been called the *"oscillating model."* This says the universe is like a spring, expanding and contracting, repeating the cycle indefinitely. The basis of this theory is that the universe is "closed"; that is, no new energy is being put into it. The expansion of matter reaches a certain point, and then the force of gravity pulls everything back together before expanding again. All the evidence, however, refutes this position. The universe is clearly losing density with no sign that the persistent expansion ever has or ever will reverse. Therefore, the universe is not closed.

Dr. William L. Craig provides the following conclusions concerning these two models: "Both the steady-state and oscillating models of the universe fail to fit the facts of observational cosmology. Therefore, we can conclude once more that the universe began to exist."[13]

• A third view of the beginning of the universe is known as the *"big bang"* theory. Dr. Edwin Hubbell plotted the speeds of the galaxies and confirmed that all the galaxies are moving apart from us and one another at enormous speeds. The law bearing his name states that the farther away a galaxy is, the faster it moves.

The staggering implication of this view is that at one time all matter was packed into a dense mass at temperatures of many trillions of degrees. Scientists who postulated this phenomenon theorize the universe must have originally resembled a white-hot fireball in the first moments after the big bang occurred.

A confirmation of this theory came in 1965 when two physicists made the startling discovery that the earth was entirely bathed in "a faint glow of radiation." Its waves followed the exact pattern of wavelength expected in a giant explosion. Since then, scientists have reconfirmed that there could be no other obvious explanation than that these radiation waves were the aftermath of the big bang.

Before the Big Bang

Dr. Robert Jastrow, who states that he is an agnostic in religious matters, comments on the theory of the big bang:

Now we see how the astronomical evidence leads to a biblical view of the origin of the world. The details differ, but the essential elements in the astronomical and biblical accounts of Genesis are the same. The chain of events leading to man commenced suddenly and sharply at a definite moment in time, in a flash of light and energy.

Scientists have traditionally rejected the thought of a natural phenomenon which cannot be explained, even with unlimited time and money. There is a kind of religion in science; every event can be explained in a rational way as the product of some previous event; every effect must have its cause. Now science has proven that the universe exploded into existence at a specific moment. It asks, "What cause produced this effect? Who or what put the matter and energy into the universe?" And science does not answer these questions.

Jastrow concludes with this monumental statement:

For the scientist who has lived by his faith in the *power of reason*, the story ends like a bad dream. He has scaled the mountains of ignorance; he is about to conquer the highest peak; as he pulls himself over the final rock, he is greeted by a band of theologians who have been sitting there for centuries.[14]

For many, this is an exceedingly strange development, unexpected by all but the theologians. They have always accepted the word of the Bible. In the beginning God created heaven and earth.

One of those theologians, David, said knowingly, "The heavens declare the glory of God; the skies proclaim the work of his hands" (Ps. 19:1). And the Apostle Paul wrote, "God has made it plain. . . . For since the creation of the world God's invisible qualities—his eternal power and divine nature—have been clearly seen, being understood from what has been made, so that men are without excuse" (Rom. 1:19-20). To which Augustine added, "Who can understand this mystery or explain it to others?"

The Moral Argument

Yet another evidence for the existence of God is what C.S. Lewis calls "right and wrong as a clue to the meaning of the universe." There is an influence or a command inside each of us trying to get us to behave in a certain way. Lewis explains that, universally, people commonly appeal to some sense of right and wrong. People argue with one another, "That's my seat. I had it first! Suppose I did the same to you! How would you like it? Come on, you promised." People make these comments every day, educated as well as uneducated, children as well as adults; all of us say these things.

In these arguments there is an appeal to some behavioral standard that the other person is assumed to accept. The person had a good reason to do it; it was OK to do it.

The appeal is to some *law or rule of fair play or morality* that's an intrinsic part of both of them. Rarely does the other person say, "Who cares about your standard?" It is there between them. They don't question it. As Lewis puts it, "Quarreling means trying to show the other man is in the wrong."

This law has to do with what ought to take place. Somehow we know it inside of us. It is not just a set of cultural norms or cultural standards. Also, there is a surprising consensus from civilization to civilization about what is moral decency. And we all do agree some moralities are better than others. "If no set of moral ideas were truer or better than any other, there would be no sense in preferring civilized morality to savage morality, or Christian morality to Nazi morality."[15]

Lewis says the moral law cannot be merely a social convention. It is more like a mathematical table, he tells us. We would never say the math table is a social convention made up to help us and which we could have made differently if we wanted to. Two plus two will always equal four irrespective of its culture.

Yes, there is Somebody behind the universe. He has put a moral law within us, and He is intensely interested in right conduct—in fair play, unselfishness, courage, good faith, honesty, and truthfulness.

God—A Celestial Killjoy?

It is important to observe here that though there are many indications of God in nature, we could never know conclusively from nature that He exists or what He is like. The question was asked centuries ago: "Can you fathom the mysteries of God?" (Job 11:7) The answer is no! Unless God reveals Himself, we are doomed to confusion and conjecture.

It is obvious that among those who believe in God there are many ideas abroad today as to what God is like. Some, for instance, believe God to be a celestial killjoy. They view Him as peering over the balcony of heaven looking for anyone who seems to be enjoying life. Then on finding such a person, He shouts down, "Cut it out!"

Others think of God as a sentimental grandfather in the sky, rocking benignly and stroking His beard as He says, "Boys will be boys." That everything will work out in the end, no matter what you have done, is conceded to be His general attitude toward people.

Others think of Him as a big ball of fire and of us as little sparks who will eventually gravitate back to the big ball. Still others, like Einstein, think of God as an impersonal force or mind. To the deist, God created the world and yet never intrudes on it; that is, He wound up the clock, and now He is letting it run down. To the theist, however, God is the Creator and Ruler, and He is personally involved in His creation while revealing Himself.

Herbert Spencer, one of the popularizers of agnosticism a century ago, observed accurately that a bird has never been known to fly out into space. Therefore, he concluded by analogy that it is impossible for the finite to penetrate the infinite; in other words, even if God does exist, we can never know Him personally or anything about His existence.

Spencer's observation was correct, but his conclusion was wrong. He missed the possibility that God, the infinite Creator could penetrate our finiteness—*the infinite could penetrate the finite*, thereby communicating to us what He is really like. This, of course, is what God did.

God Has Penetrated the Finite

As the writer to the Hebrews puts it: "In the past God spoke to our fore-fathers through the prophets at many times and in various ways, but in these last days he has spoken to us by his Son, whom he appointed heir of all things, and through whom he made the universe" (Heb. 1:1-2).

Throughout history, God has taken the initiative to communicate to humankind. His fullest revelation has been His invasion into human history in the person of Jesus Christ. Here, in terms of human personality we can understand that God has lived among us.

If you wanted to communicate your love to a colony of ants, how could you most effectively do it? Clearly, it would be best to become an ant. Only in this way could your existence and what you were like be communicated fully and effectively. This is what God did with us. We are, as J.B. Phillips aptly put it, "The Visited Planet." The best and clearest answer to how we know there is a God is that He has visited us. The other indications are merely clues or hints. What confirms them conclusively is the birth, life, death, and resurrection of Jesus Christ.

INVISIBLE does not mean UNREAL.

Changed Lives

Other evidence for the reality of God's existence is His clear presence in the lives of men and women today. When Jesus Christ is believed and trusted, a profound change takes place in the individual, and ultimately, the community. One of the most moving illustrations of this is recorded by Ernest Gordon, former chaplain at Princeton University. In his *Through the Valley of the Kwai*, he tells how the prisoners of the Japanese on the Malay Peninsula during World War II had been reduced almost to animals, stealing food from their buddies, who were also starving. In their desperation, the prisoners decided it would be good to read the New Testament.

Because Gordon was a university graduate, they asked him to lead. By his own admission he was a skeptic, and those who asked him to lead them were nonbelievers too. He and others came to trust Christ when they became acquainted with Him in all of His beauty and power through the uncluttered simplicity of the New Testament. How this group of scrounging, clawing humans was transformed into a community of love is a touching and powerful story that clearly demonstrates the reality of God in Jesus Christ. Although in less dramatic terms, many others today have experienced this same reality.

There is, then, convincing evidence from creation, history, and contemporary life that there is a God and that this God can be known in one's personal experience.

Is Christ God?

I t is impossible for us to know conclusively whether God exists and what He is like—unless *He* takes the initiative and *He* reveals Himself. Without His initiative and self-revelation we are left to conjecture, unfounded opinion, or prejudice. Legitimately, we ask what He is like and what His attitude toward us is. If we were certain He existed but learned He was like Adolf Hitler—capricious, vicious, prejudiced, and cruel—what a horrible realization that would be!

A brief scan of the horizon of history gives us some clue to God personally revealing Himself. One clear clue stands out. In an obscure village in Palestine, almost 2,000 years ago, a child was born in a stable. The reigning monarch in that territory feared the birth of this child, who was prophesied to be "king of the Jews." In an attempt to murder this baby and remove this threat to his crown, King Herod gave orders to kill all the boys two years old and younger who were born in Bethlehem. In vain he hoped to destroy this infant rival. Historians have called that horrible event the "slaughter of the innocents" (Matt. 2:1-18).

His birth split time in two! Indeed, the life of this child was destined to change the course of history. Two thousand years ago, His coming rocked the world. It changed the calendar and tailored people's mores. The atheist dates his checks with the current year, in effect, declaring His birth. The rulers of countries, both East and West and regardless of their religions, use His birth date. Unthinkingly, we declare His birth on letters, legal documents, and date books. At this writing, it's been 1,999 years since Jesus Christ was born. On His birth date, the mall parking lots are still starkly empty, silent evidence of His coming to earth.

Going back those twenty centuries, we find the baby, whose name was Jesus, and His parents settling in Nazareth, where He learned His earthly father's trade of carpentry. From the beginning He was an unusual child. When He was twelve years old, He confounded the scholars and rabbis in the Jerusalem synagogue. His parents remonstrated with Him because He had stayed behind after they had departed from the holy city, but He made the mystifying reply when they found Him: "Didn't you know I had to be in my Father's [God's] house?" (Luke 2:49). His answer implied a unique relationship between Himself and God.

This young man lived in obscurity until He was thirty, and then He began a public ministry lasting three years. He was known as a kindly person, and we are told "the common people heard him gladly." He stood out in a way that was unlike all other teachers: "He taught as one who had authority, and not as their teachers of the law" (Matt. 7:29).

Jesus Claimed to Be the Son of God

It soon became apparent, however, that Jesus was making shocking and startling statements about Himself. He began to identify Himself as far more than a remarkable teacher or an exceptional prophet. He clearly asserted His deity, and He made His identity the focal point of His teaching. The all-important question Jesus put to those who followed Him was "Who do you say I am?" (Matt. 16:15) Peter, His devoted disciple, answered, "You are the Christ, the Son of the living God" (v. 16). Peter's declaration did not shock Jesus, nor did the Lord rebuke His friend. On the contrary, Jesus commended Peter.

In fact, Jesus explicitly claimed to be the Son of God. It is clear that His hearers got the full impact of His words. We are told, "The Jews tried all the harder to kill him; not only was he breaking the Sabbath, but he was even calling God his own Father, making himself equal with God" (John 5:18).

On another occasion Jesus said, "I and the Father are one" (John 10:30). Immediately the Jews wanted to stone Him. He asked them for which good work they wanted to kill Him. They replied, "We are not stoning you for any of these," they replied, "but for blasphemy, because you, a mere man, claim to be God" (v. 33).

Jesus claimed and demonstrated the attributes that only God has.

> **Christianity is not a PATH, but a PERSON, not RULES, but a RELATIONSHIP.**

When a paralytic was let down through a roof and placed at His feet, Jesus said, "Son, your sins are forgiven" (Mark 2:5). This caused a great ruckus among the scribes, who said in their hearts, "Why does this fellow talk like that? He's blaspheming! Who can forgive sins but God alone?" (v. 7)

Jesus, knowing their thoughts, said to them, "Which is easier: to say to the paralytic, 'Your sins are forgiven,' or to say, 'Get up, take your mat and walk'?" (v. 9) Jesus then answered their question: "That you may know that the Son of Man has authority on earth to forgive sins [in effect, You rightly say God alone can forgive sins, but since this cannot be seen, I will do something you can see]" (v. 10). Turning to the palsied man, Jesus commanded him, "I tell you, get up, take your mat and go home" (v. 11). The man got up and walked! Thus Jesus proved His deity by demonstrating His divine power.

The title *Son of Man* is a title Jesus used to refer to Himself, but always with some assertion of deity. In His words concerning His coming Jesus speaks of Himself as the Son of Man who came "to give his life a ransom for many." This is not a disclaimer of deity, by any means. Rather the title embraces both His deity *and* His coming as a part of the human race. His authority, miracles, teaching, sinlessness, and character were traits true only of God.

At the critical moment when His life was at stake because of these claims, the high priest put the question to Him directly: "Are you the Christ, the Son of the Blessed One?" "I am," said Jesus calmly, "and you will see the Son of Man sitting at the right hand of the Mighty One [God] and coming on the clouds of heaven." The high priest tore his clothes and asked, "Why do we need any more witnesses? . . . You have heard the blasphemy" (Mark 14:61-64).

John Stott sums up the deity of Christ as seen in His everyday actions, "So close was his connection with God that he equated a man's attitude to Himself with the man's attitude to God. Thus, to know Him was to know God (John 8:19; 14:7). To see Him was to see God (12:45; 14:9). To believe in him was to believe in God (12:44; 14:1). To receive him was to receive God (Mark 9:37). To hate him was to hate God (John 15:23). And to honor him was to honor God (v. 23)."[1]

Only Four Possibilities

As we deal with Jesus Christ's claim that He is God, there are only four possibilities open to us. He was either a liar, a lunatic, a legend, or the Truth. If we say Jesus is not the Truth, our reasoning has to take us automatically to affirming one of the other three alternatives, whether we realize it or not. Therefore, we must examine these possibilities carefully and objectively to determine which is true.

1. *Did Jesus lie when He claimed to be God while knowing He was not God?* If so, Jesus deliberately deceived His listeners in order to lend authority to Himself and His teaching. Few, if any, seriously hold this position. Even those who deny His deity affirm Jesus as "a great moral teacher." They seemingly fail to realize, however, that those two views contradict each other. Jesus could hardly be a great moral teacher if, on the most crucial point of His teaching—His identity—He was a deliberate liar.

2. *Was Jesus a lunatic?* In order to take this position we would have to considerably contort the evidence concerning Jesus' life. In fact, there is no evidence to support this view. Rather, all the evidence points in the other direction—that He was very much sane and rational throughout His life. It may seem kinder, though no less shocking, to say Jesus was sincere but self-deceived. A person today who thinks he is God or a fried taco might be unkindly designated as "lunatic"—someone we would want to help. However, the term would be ludicrous if applied to Jesus Christ.

As we look at the life of Christ, we see no evidence of the psychological abnormality and imbalance common in a deranged person. Rather, we find the greatest composure under pressure. A perfect example of Jesus' composure was at His trial before Pilate. When His very life was at stake, Jesus was calm and serene. As C.S. Lewis put it, "The discrepancy between the depth and sanity of His moral teaching and a diagnosis of rampant megalomania" are patently incompatible.[2]

3. *Was Jesus a legend?* This third alternative view asserts that Jesus' claim to be divine and the description of His supernatural power were the invention of His enthusiastic followers, and therefore are a legend. It has even been rumored that His claim to be God, the teachings He gave, and His miracles were added to the accounts about Jesus up until the third and fourth centuries. Words were put into His mouth that He would have been shocked to hear. Were He to return He would immediately repudiate them. So they say.

Modern archaeological discoveries, however, have significantly refuted the legend theory. In fact, three statements emerge after examining these discoveries that undermine this theory.

• It has been conclusively proven that the four biographies of Jesus (Matthew, Mark, Luke, and John) were written within the lifetime of contemporaries of Christ, who would have dismissed such teachings were they false.

• "There is no reason to believe that any of the Gospels were written later than A.D. 70," concluded Dr. William F. Albright, world-famous archaeologist now retired from Johns Hopkins University.

• For a mere legend about Christ in the form of the Gospel to have gained the circulation and to have had the impact it had without one shred of basis in fact would be simply incredible.

For this to have happened would be as fantastic as for someone in our own time to write a biography of the late John F. Kennedy and in it say he claimed to be God, to forgive people's sins, and to have risen from the dead. Such a story is so preposterous it would never get off the ground because there are still too many people around who knew Kennedy! The legend theory does not hold water in the light of the logic and early date of the Gospel manuscripts.

4. *Jesus spoke the Truth—He was God come to earth.* From one point of view, claims don't mean much. Talk is cheap. Anyone can make claims, and many could be named from around the world. I could claim to be God, and you could claim to be God, but the question all of us must answer is "What credentials do we bring to substantiate our claim?" In my case it wouldn't take five minutes to disprove my claim. It probably wouldn't take too much longer to dispose of yours.

But when it comes to Jesus of Nazareth, it's not that simple. He had the credentials to back up His claim. He said, "Even though you do not believe me, believe the miracles, that you may know and understand that the Father is in me, and I in the Father" (John 10:38).

What Were Jesus' Credentials?

• First, His moral character coincided with His claims. When we read about any delusioned person who claims to be God, we know their character undermines their claim. No one argues this fact. Not so with Christ, however. We do not compare Christ with others. In fact, we contrast all others with Him. He is unique—as unique as God.

Jesus Christ was sinless. The caliber of His life was such that He was able to challenge His enemies with the question: "Can any of you prove me guilty of sin?" (John 8:46) He was met by silence even though He had addressed those who wanted nothing more than to point out a flaw in His character.

• Second, we read of the temptations of Jesus, but we never hear of a confession of sin on His part. He never asked for forgiveness, although He told His followers to do so.

This lack of any sense of moral failure on Jesus' part is completely contrary to the accounts of the saints and mystics in all ages. The closer men and women draw to God, the more overwhelmed they are with their own failure, corruption, and shortcomings. This is also true for ordinary mortals in the moral realm. The closer one is to a shining light, the more he realizes his need for a bath.

• Third, His followers, such as Peter, John, and Paul, all of whom were trained from earliest childhood to believe in the universality of sin, clearly spoke of the sinlessness of Jesus: "He committed no sin, and no deceit was found in his mouth" (1 Peter 2:22); "In him is no sin" (1 John 3:5); Jesus "had no sin" (2 Cor. 5:21).

Even Pilate, who certainly was not a friend of Jesus, said, "I find no basis for a charge against him" (John 18:38). He implicitly recognized Christ's innocence. And the Roman centurion who witnessed the death of Christ exclaimed, "Surely he was the Son of God!" (Matt. 27:54)

In Jesus Christ we find the perfect personality. Bernard Ramm writes:

> If God were a man, we would expect His personality to be true humanity. Only God could tell us what a true man should be like. Certainly there are forerunners of piety in Old Testament models. Foremost must be a complete consciousness, coupled with a complete dedication and consecration of life to God. Then, ranked below this, are the other virtues, graces, and attributes that characterize perfect humanity. Intelligence must not stifle piety, and prayer must not be a substitute for work, and zeal must not be irrational fanaticism, and reserve must not become stolidity.

And in the same book John Schaff comments:

> Jesus' zeal never degenerated into passion, nor his constancy into obstinacy, nor his benevolence into weakness, nor his tenderness into sentimentality. His unworldliness was free from indifference and unsociableness or undue familiarity; his self-denial from moroseness; his temperance from austerity. He combined childlike innocency with manly strength, absorbing devotion to God with untiring interest in the welfare of man, tender love to the sinner with uncompromising severity against sin, commanding dignity with winning humility, fearless courage with wise caution, unyielding firmness with sweet gentleness![3]

> **JESUS SAID HE WAS THE ONLY WAY TO GOD. One way is not narrow if it's the TRUE way.**
>
> **The airline pilot can land on only ONE runway.**
>
> **In the United States there is only ONE right side of the road to drive on.**

• Fourth, Christ demonstrated a

power over natural forces, which could belong only to God, the Author of these forces.

He stilled a raging storm of wind and waves on the Sea of Galilee. In doing this, He provoked from those in the boat the awestruck question: "Who is this? Even the wind and the waves obey him!" (Mark 4:41) He turned water into wine and fed 5,000 people from five loaves and two fish. He gave a grieving widow back her only son by raising him from the dead and brought to life the dead daughter of a shattered father. To a friend He said, "Lazarus, come forth!" and dramatically raised him from the dead. It is most significant that Jesus' enemies did not deny this miracle. Rather, they tried to kill Him. "If we let him go on like this," they said, "everyone will believe in him" (John 11:48).

• Fifth, Jesus demonstrated the Creator's power over sickness and disease. He made the lame to walk, the dumb to speak, and the blind to see. Some of His healings were congenital problems not susceptible to psychosomatic cure. The most outstanding was that of the blind man whose case is recorded in John 9. Though the man couldn't answer his skeptical questioners, his experience was enough to convince him. "One thing I do know. I was blind but now I see!" he declared (John 9:25). He was astounded that the religious leaders didn't recognize his healer as the Son of God. "Nobody has ever heard of opening the eyes of a man born blind," he said (v. 32). To him the evidence was as obvious as his sight.

• Sixth, Jesus' supreme credential to authenticate His claim to deity was His resurrection from the dead.

Five times in the course of His life He predicted He would die. He also predicted how He would die and that three days later He would rise from the dead and appear to His disciples (see Matt. 16:21; 17:22-23; Mark 8:31; 10:32-33; Luke 9:22). Surely this was the great test. It was a claim that was easy to verify. It either happened or it didn't.

The Resurrection is so crucial and foundational a subject we will devote an entire chapter to it. If the Resurrection happened, there is no difficulty with any other miracles. And if we establish the Resurrection, we have the answer to the big question concerning God, His character, and our relationship to Him. An answer to this question makes it possible to answer all subsidiary questions.

Christ moved history as only God could do. Schaff portrays Jesus this way:

This Jesus of Nazareth without money and arms conquered more millions than Alexander, Caesar, Muhammad and Napoleon; without science and learning, he shed more light on matters human and divine than all philosophers and scholars combined; without the eloquence of schools, he spoke such words of life as were never spoken before or since and produced effects which lie beyond the reach of orator or poet; without writing a single line, he set more pens in motion and furnished themes for more sermons, orations, discussions, learned volumes, works of art and songs of praise than the whole army of great men of ancient and modern times.[4]

• Seventh, and finally, we know that Christ is God because we can experience Him today.

Experience in itself is not conclusive, but combined with the historical reality of Jesus' resurrection it gives us the basis for our solid conviction. There is no other hypothesis to explain all the data we have than the profound fact that Jesus Christ is God the Son.

Did Christ Rise
from the Dead?

B oth friends and enemies of Christianity have recognized that the resurrection of Jesus Christ is the foundation stone of the faith. In the early church at Corinth some were questioning, even denying the possibility of the resurrection of the dead. Hearing this, the Apostle Paul gave the astute summary statement: "If Christ has not been raised, our preaching is useless and so is your faith" (1 Cor. 15:14). With these few words, Paul soundly rested his whole case on the bodily resurrection of Jesus Christ. Either Jesus did or did not rise from the dead. If He did, it was the most sensational event in all of history, and it gives us conclusive answers to the most profound questions of our existence:

- Where have we come from?
- Why are we here?
- What is our future destiny?

If Christ rose, we know with certainty that God exists, what He is like, and that He cares for each of us individually. The universe, therefore, takes on meaning and purpose, and we can experience the living God in contemporary life. These and many other life-expanding things are true if Jesus of Nazareth rose from the dead.

Not Wishful Thinking

On the other hand, if Christ did not rise from the dead, Christianity is an interesting museum piece, but nothing more. It has no objective validity or reality. Though it is a nice wishful thought, it certainly isn't worth getting steamed up about. How sad that the martyrs in the early centuries went unwaveringly into the den of lions, singing as they

> **We can connect with Him. He is ALIVE!**

went! In this century nationals and missionaries on other continents have given their lives uselessly and have been poor deluded fools.

Attacks on Christianity by dissenters have most often concentrated on the Resurrection. A remarkable plan of assault was contemplated in the early 1930s by a young British lawyer, convinced the Resurrection was mere fable, and intent to do the world a favor by once and for all exposing this fraud and superstition. As a lawyer, he felt he had the critical faculties to sift data and admit nothing as evidence that did not meet the stiff criteria for admission into today's law court.

However, while Frank Morison was doing his research, a remarkable thing happened. The case was not nearly as easy as he had supposed. As a result, the first chapter in his book *Who Moved the Stone?* is titled "The Book That Refused to Be Written." In it he described how, as he examined the evidence, he became persuaded against his will that the bodily Resurrection was fact.

Data to Be Considered

What are some of the pieces of data pertinent to the Resurrection when examining the question: "Did Christ rise from the dead?"

• *First, the existence of the Christian church is a fact.* It is worldwide in scope. Its history can be traced back to Palestine around A.D. 32. The Acts of the Apostles is a litany of stories relating how the message of Jesus and His resurrection stirred whole communities. The believers were first called Christians in the city of Antioch. In Thessalonica Paul's preaching persuaded some of the Jews, a large number of God-fearing Greeks, and not a few prominent women to believe. The message literally "turned the world upside down" (Acts 17:6, KJV). Jesus' followers constantly referred to the Resurrection as the basis for their teaching, preaching, living, and—significantly—dying.

• *Second, the Christian day is a fact; that is, Sunday is the day of worship for Christians.* Its history can also be traced back to the year A.D. 32. Such a shift in the calendar was monumental. Something cataclysmic must have happened to change the day of worship from the Jewish Sabbath, the seventh day of the week, to Sunday, the first day. The writer of Acts 20:7 simply stated, "On the first day of the week we came together," which has become an established pattern. Christians said the shift came because of their desire to celebrate the day Jesus rose from the dead. This shift is all the more remarkable when we remember that the first Christians were Jews. If the Resurrection does not account for this change, what does?

• *Third, there is Christian Scripture—the New Testament.* In its pages are contained independent testimonies to the fact of the Resurrection. At least three of these were eyewitnesses: John, Peter, and Matthew. In addition, Luke's Gospel gives evidence of Jesus' resurrection by a historian with a classical background known to have traveled with Paul and to have heard him preach the Resurrection (2 Tim. 4:11). In fact, writing to the churches at an early date, Paul referred to the Resurrection in such a way that it is obvious to him and his readers the event was well known and accepted without question.

Are these men who helped transform the moral structure of society consummate liars or deluded madmen? These possibilities stem from our knowledge of people of questionable character, but knowing what Jesus' followers did and what they taught and what they died for, it is far harder to believe that they were liars or madmen than it is to believe their account of Jesus, the incarnation of God, rising from the dead. Indeed, there is not a shred of evidence to support the view that the New Testament writers were liars or were mad.

For intelligent belief, two facets of the Resurrection require explanation by believer and nonbeliever alike. They are the empty tomb and the alleged appearances of Jesus Christ following His burial.

Accounting for the Empty Tomb

• *The earliest explanation circulated was that the disciples stole the body!* In Matthew 28:11-15, we have the record of the reaction of the chief priests and the elders when the guards gave them the infuriating and mysterious news that Jesus' body was gone after His burial. These religious leaders gave the soldiers money and told them to say the disciples had come at night and stolen the body while they were asleep. This story was so obviously false Matthew didn't even bother to refute it! What judge would listen to you if you said your neighbor came into your house and stole your television set while you were asleep? How would you know it was your neighbor if you were asleep? Testimony like this would be laughed out of any court.

Furthermore, we are faced with a psychological and ethical impossibility. Stealing the body of Christ is something totally foreign to the character of the disciples and all we know of them. It would mean they were perpetrators of a deliberate lie resulting in the deception and ultimate death of thousands of people. It is inconceivable that even a few of the disciples could have conspired together and pulled off a theft of the body and never have told the others.

Moreover, every one of the disciples faced the test of torture, and all but the Apostle John were martyred for their teachings and beliefs. People will die for what they believe to be true, though it may actually be false. They do not, however, die for what they know is a lie. If ever a person tells the truth, it is on his or her deathbed, and there is no evidence that any of Jesus' disciples changed his account of Jesus' resurrection, including before his death.

• *A second hypothesis is that the authorities, Jewish or Roman, moved the body.* But why? Having put special Roman guards at the tomb, what would the Romans gain by moving the body? The convincing answer for this thesis is the silence of these authorities in the face of the apostles' bold preaching in Jerusalem about the Resurrection. The ecclesiastical leaders were seething with rage and did everything possible to prevent the spread of this message and to suppress it (Acts 4). They arrested Peter and John. Then they beat and threatened them in an attempt to close their mouths.

For either the Jewish or Roman authorities, there was a very simple solution to their problem. If either of them had Christ's body, they could have paraded it through the streets of Jerusalem. In one fell swoop they would have successfully smothered Christianity in its cradle. That they did not do this bears eloquent testimony to the fact that they did not have the body.

• *Another popular theory, called the wrong tomb theory, suggests that the distraught women, overcome with grief, missed their way in the dimness of the morning.* In their distress they imagined Christ had risen because the tomb was empty.

This theory, however, falls because of the same argument that destroys the previous one. If the women had gone to the wrong tomb, why did the high priests and other enemies of the faith not go to the right tomb and produce the body? Furthermore, it is inconceivable that all of Jesus' followers would have committed the same mistake. Certainly Joseph of Arimathea, owner of the tomb, would have solved the problem. In addition, it must be remembered that this was a private burial ground, not a public cemetery, as we envision it. There was no other tomb nearby that would have allowed them to make this mistake.

• *The swoon theory has also been advanced to explain the empty tomb.* In this view, Christ did not actually die. He was mistakenly reported to be dead but had passed out from exhaustion, pain, and loss of blood. When He was laid in the coolness of the tomb, He revived. He came out of the tomb and appeared to His disciples, and they mistakenly thought He had risen from the dead.

This theory is of modern construction. It first appeared at the end of the eighteenth century. It is significant that not a suggestion of this kind has come down from antiquity among all the violent attacks that have been made against Christianity. All of the earliest records are emphatic about Jesus' death and shedding of blood.

For a moment, let us assume Christ swooned and was buried alive. Is it possible to believe He would have survived burial in a damp tomb without food or water or attention of any kind? Would He have survived being wrapped in seventy-five pounds of spice-laden graveclothes? Would He have had the strength to extricate Himself from the graveclothes, push the heavy stone away from the mouth of the grave, overcome the Roman guards, and walk miles on feet that had been pierced with spikes? Then, at that point, would He have the strength to present Himself as a glorious and majestic God to be worshiped? Such a belief is more fantastic than the simple fact of the Resurrection itself.

Even the German critic David Strauss, who by no means believes in the Resurrection, rejected this idea as incredible. He said,

> It is impossible that One who had just come forth from the grave half dead, who crept about weak and ill, who stood in the need of medical treatment, of bandaging, strengthening, and tender care, and who at last succumbed to suffering, could ever have given the disciples the impression that he was a conqueror over death and the grave; that he was the Prince of Life. This lay at the bottom of their future ministry. Such a resuscitation could only have weakened the impression which He had made upon them in life and in death—or at the most, could have given it an elegiac voice—but could by no possibility have changed their sorrow into enthusiasm or elevated their reverence into worship.[1]

Finally, if this theory is correct, Christ Himself was involved in flagrant lies. His disciples believed and preached it—He was dead but came alive again. Jesus did nothing to dispel this belief, but rather encouraged it.

The only theory that adequately explains the empty tomb is the resurrection of Jesus Christ from the dead. With other religionists, their tombs become shrines of worship. With Christ, however, the empty tomb is a place where Christians rejoice.

The Appearances of Christ

The second piece of data that both believer and nonbeliever must explain is the recorded appearances of Christ. Ten distinct appearances are recorded. These occurred from the morning of His resurrection to His ascension forty days later. They show great variety as to time, place, and people. Two were to individuals, Peter and James. Other appearances were to the disciples as a group, and one was to 500 assembled believers. They were each one at different places. Some were in the garden near His tomb, and some were in the Upper Room. One was on the road from Jerusalem to Emmaus, and some were far away in Galilee. Each appearance was characterized by different acts and words by Jesus.

Lies or legends cannot explain the empty tomb, nor can we dismiss the appearances of Jesus Christ on this kind of basis. The accounts are testimonies given by eyewitnesses—people who were there, had seen and interacted with Him, and were profoundly certain of the truth of their statements.

Logically, one might propose hallucinations to discount these eyewitness accounts of Christ's appearances after crucifixion. At first, this sounds like a plausible explanation of an otherwise supernatural event. It is plausible until we remember the common laws observed by modern medicine, which apply to such psychological phenomena. As we relate these principles to the evidence at hand, we can see what at first seemed most plausible is, in fact, impossible.

> # Jesus Christ's life, death, and resurrection assure us:
>
> - **His purpose is to "rescue us" from sin.**
>
> - **His power will give us "eternal life."**
>
> - **His suffering demonstrates the extent of His love for us.**

Hallucinations generally occur in people who tend to be vividly imaginative and of a nervous makeup. But the appearances of Christ were to all sorts of people. True, some were sensitive, but there were also hardheaded fishermen like Peter and others of various dispositions.

Hallucinations are known to be extremely subjective and individual. For this reason, no two people have the same experience. In the case of the Resurrection, Christ appeared not just to individuals but also to groups, including one with more than 500 people. When Paul wrote his first letter to the Christians in Corinth, he said more than half of those people were still alive and could tell about these events (1 Cor. 15).

Hallucinations usually occur only at particular times and places, and they are associated with the events fancied. However, these appearances occurred both indoors and outdoors, and in the morning, afternoon, and evening.

In general, psychic experiences occur over a long period of time and with some regularity. These appearances happened during a period of forty days, and then stopped abruptly. No one ever said they happened again.

Perhaps the most conclusive indication of the fallacy of the hallucination theory is a fact often overlooked. In order to have an experience like this, one must so intensely want to believe that he or she projects something that really isn't there and attaches reality to this imagination. For instance, a mother who has lost a son in the war remembers how he used to come home from work every evening at 5:30. She sits in her rocking chair every afternoon, musing and meditating. Finally, she thinks she sees him come through the door and has a conversation with him. At this point she has lost contact with reality.

Persuaded against Their Wills

One might think hallucination is what happened to the disciples regarding the Resurrection. The fact is the opposite took place—they were persuaded against their wills that Jesus had risen from the dead!

• Mary came to the tomb on the first Easter Sunday morning with spices in her hands. Why? To anoint the dead body of the Lord she loved. She was obviously not expecting to find Him risen from the dead. In fact, when she first saw Him she mistook Him for the gardener! It was only after He spoke to her and spoke her name that she realized who He was.

• When the other disciples heard, they didn't believe. The story seemed to them "as an idle tale."

• When the resurrected Jesus finally appeared to the disciples, they were frightened and thought they were seeing a ghost! They thought they were having a hallucination, and it jolted them. To convince them, Jesus finally said, "Touch me and see; a ghost does not have flesh and bones, as you see I have" (Luke 24:39). He asked them if they had any food, and they gave Him a piece of broiled fish. Luke

> "This is how God showed his love among us: he sent his one and only Son into the world that we might live through him."
>
> **1 John 4:9**

didn't add the obvious—ghosts don't eat fish!

• Finally, there is the classic case which remains in our language today—"doubting Thomas." Thomas, one of the apostles, was not present when Jesus appeared to the disciples the first time. They told Thomas about it, but he scoffed and would not believe them. In effect, he said, "I'm from Missouri. I won't believe unless I'm shown. I'm an empiricist. Unless I can put my finger into the nail wounds in His hands and my hand into His side, I will not believe." He wasn't about to succumb to a hallucination! Yet John gives us the graphic story of Jesus' appearance to the disciples a week later (John 20). The Lord graciously invited Thomas to examine the evidence of His hands and His side. Thomas looked at Him and fell down in worship: "My Lord and my God!" (v. 28)

To hold the hallucination theory in explaining the appearances of Christ, one must completely ignore the evidence.

What was it that changed a band of frightened, cowardly disciples into men of courage and conviction? What was it that changed Peter, who was so afraid for his own skin the night before the crucifixion that he publicly denied three times that he even knew Jesus? Some fifty days later he became a roaring lion, risking his life by saying he had seen Jesus risen from the dead. It must be remembered that Peter preached his electric Pentecost sermon in Jerusalem, where all these events took place, thus putting himself in grave danger. He was not in Galilee, miles away where no one could verify the facts and where his ringing statements might go unchallenged.

Only the bodily resurrection of Christ could have produced this astounding change in Peter.

Contemporary Proof

Finally, there is the evidence for the Resurrection, which is contemporary and personal. If Jesus Christ rose from the dead, He is alive today, ready to invade and change those who invite Him into their lives. Thousands now living bear testimony to the fact that Jesus Christ has revolutionized their lives. He has transformed them as He had promised He would. The proof of the pudding is in the eating. The invitation still stands, "Taste and see that the Lord is good!" (Ps. 34:8) The avenue to accept the offer to connect with the living Christ is open to all.

In summary, then, we can agree with Canon Westcott, a brilliant scholar at Cambridge, who said, "Indeed, taking all the evidence togeth-er, it is not too much to say there is no historic incident better or more variously supported than the resurrection of Christ. Nothing but the antecedent assumption that it must be false could have suggested the idea of deficiency in the proof of it."[2]

Is the Bible God's Word?

I heard about a Christian family who prayed out loud together several times each day. One day the youngest son looked up at a picture of Jesus on the kitchen wall, stared at it, and said thoughtfully, "Jesus, Jesus, Jesus. That's all I hear. But He don't say nothin' back!"

Fortunately for us, Jesus does say something back . . . in the Bible. The Apostle Peter tells us God has communicated "everything we need for life and godliness through our knowledge of him [Jesus Christ]" (2 Peter 1:3). When we contemplate this holy book as containing all God wants us to know for godliness, our perspective can change. This is not an insignificant book. "Read the instructions," our Designer reminds us. Still it is valid to ask, "Is the Bible God's Word? How do we know the Bible in its totality is God speaking?"

As important as those questions are, the starting point is to understand the Bible's overall message. From the beginning, its message recounts God's actions in creating our world, His character and His initiative toward the people He created. "God has spoken" are the words frequently used (Hebrews 11:1). The entire 66 books hang together revealing our Creator's love and plan for a relationship with each of us. Think for a moment, the God of heaven has a message for you. Therefore, let it inflame your interest.

As a beginning, read the Bible, starting with the New Testament. Ask some questions such as, What is behind the stories, the histories, the interventions of God? What do the four Gospels—Matthew, Mark, Luke, and John—tell us about Jesus Christ? Who is He? What is He like? This Book is our source.

As we explore the four Gospels, the life of Jesus Christ unfolds for us: His miraculous acts, His kindly relationships with people, His extraordinary definition of Himself, and finally His self-predicted death and resurrection. The four Gospels recounting Jesus' life are "the inviolate genes of the Christian faith," says Malcolm Muggeridge. "To the glory of these words majestic buildings were built, Bach composed, El Greco painted, St. Augustine labored at his *City of God* and Pascal wrote his *Pénsees.* And in them Bunyan found his inspiration in describing a Pilgrim's journey through the wilderness of this world."[1]

But how can we know for ourselves that the events and thoughts in this Book are really divine, that they are from God Himself? For a starter, the Bible describes itself as the uniquely inspired Word of God. While this claim alone is not final proof, it's a significant piece of data that cannot be ignored. An example of this logic would be in our own court systems. We take into consideration as vital evidence when a person on trial declares his or her innocence. The Bible emphatically states in numerous ways its words are God's words. It is major evidence to be considered.

No Ordinary Book

As we read the biblical narratives and histories, it will be obvious that Scripture is not like an ordinary textbook or philosophical treatise, such as those written by Socrates or Plato. In fact, the authors of the Old Testament called this holy book "the Word of God" 394 times and used various synonyms such as law, statutes, precepts, commands, ordinances, and decrees to describe it.[2] Furthermore, the writers of the New Testament regularly referred to the Old Testament as the "Word of God." Interestingly, the psalmist declared, "I have hidden your word in my heart that I might not sin against you" (Ps. 119:11). This psalm is a model of literary genius with an alphabetic acrostic devoting eight verses to each of the twenty-one letters in the Hebrew alphabet—a total of

176 verses. All but one or two verses refer to the "Word of God" in some form or another.

Although about forty authors wrote the Bible, this book shows a single theme, which focuses on God's creation of and relationship with humankind. This thread of interaction is woven throughout the entire book from beginning to end. The earliest of the sixty-six books was first authored about 1100 B.C. and the last one, Revelation, was finished about one hundred years after Jesus' birth. Every one of the authors contributed to this single, focused perspective: the will, plan, and covenant of God with humanity.

Beethoven Was Not "God-Breathed"

This is how the Bible describes itself: "All Scripture is God-breathed and is useful for teaching, rebuking, correcting and training in righteousness" (2 Tim. 3:16).

The word *God-breathed*, or *inspired* as other versions translate it, is not to be confused with the common usage of the word, as when we say Shakespeare was inspired and wrote great plays, or Beethoven was inspired and composed great symphonies. In the biblical sense inspiration is unique. Indeed, God was the primary author of the Bible; He was the One who inspired the writers to speak truths. He was the initiator, if you will. Whereas God was the source, the writers were the recipients. This point is extremely important to grasp.

The Apostle Peter said it pointedly. The Old Testament "prophecy never had its origin in the will of man, but men spoke from God as they were *carried along* by the Holy Spirit" (2 Peter 1:21, italics added). The Bible is the product of God Himself. The ideas are not mere human thoughts but come from God's will, and His divine character is revealed through human words.

Nevertheless, the writers of Scripture were not mere writing machines. God did not punch them, like keys on a keyboard, to produce His message. He did not dictate the words, as some have caricatured the biblical view of inspiration. It is quite clear that each writer had a style of his own. Jeremiah did not write as Isaiah did, and John did not write as Paul did. God worked through each personality of the people He chose to be His instrument, guiding and directing them that what they wrote was *what He wanted written.*

Indications of Supernatural Origin

The Bible is the true word of God regardless of one's opinion of it.
Merely believing the Bible doesn't make it true.
Disbelieving it doesn't make it untrue.

From beginning to end there are intimations of the Bible's claim to a supernatural origin.

• The prophets and other writers were consciously aware that they were God's mouthpieces. "The word of the Lord came to me" is a phrase that recurs frequently in the Old Testament. David declared, "The Spirit of the Lord spoke through me; his word was on my tongue" (2 Sam. 23:2). Jeremiah said, "The Lord reached out his hand and touched my mouth and said to me, 'Now, I have put my words in your mouth'" (Jer. 1:9).

When later writers of Scripture quoted parts of the Bible previously recorded, they frequently referred to the prophetic writings as words spoken by God rather than by that particular prophet. For instance, Paul wrote, "The Scripture foresaw that God would justify the Gentiles by faith, and announced the gospel in advance to Abraham: 'All nations will be blessed through you'" (Gal. 3:8).

• Scripture itself is identified with God in several biblical passages. For example, "Sovereign Lord . . . you spoke by the Holy Spirit through the mouth of your servant, our father David: 'Why do the nations rage and the peoples plot in vain?'" (Acts 4:24-25, quoting Ps. 2:1) Benjamin Warfield points out that what is assumed in these two passages in the Scriptures is that the source for these biblical words is God Himself. The result from such a habitual identification of God with Scripture in the minds of the biblical writers could only be that God spoke the scriptural text. It became natural, therefore, to use the phrase "Scripture says" and the phrase "God says" when what was really intended was "Scripture, the Word of God, says. . . ." The two sets of passages, together, thus show an absolute identification of Scripture with the speaking God.[3]

• The New Testament writers were equally clear in their claim to have the same prophetic authority as the Old Testament writers. Jesus said John the Baptist was a prophet and more than a prophet (Matt. 11:9-15). Gordon Clark affirms this point by saying, "The New Testament prophets were no less inspired than their Old Testament forerunners."[4]

In fact, Paul claimed prophetic authority: "If anybody thinks he is a prophet or spiritually gifted, let him acknowledge that what I am writing to you is the Lord's command" (1 Cor. 14:37). Admit that his words come from God, he asserted, not from himself.

Peter spoke of Paul's letters as that "which ignorant and unstable people distort, as they do the other Scriptures, to their own destruction" (2 Peter 3:16). His reference to them on the same level as "the other Scriptures" shows that he viewed Paul's words as having the prophetic authority of Scripture.

Jesus' View of Scripture

Most significant of all, however, is Jesus' view of Scripture. What did He think of it? How did He use it? If we can answer these questions, we will have the answer from the One the Bible sets forth as "the Word became flesh." He was the One spoken of in both the Old and New Testament,

EVENTS PREDICTED AND FULFILLED IN JESUS' LIFE		
Event in Jesus' Life	**Old Testament**	**Prophecy Fulfilled**
Born in Bethlehem	Micah 5:2	Luke 2:4-7
Sold for 30 pieces of silver	Zech. 11:13	Matt. 26:15
Silver used to buy a potter's field	Zech. 11:13	Matt. 27:6
Silent when accused	Isa. 53:7	Matt. 27:12-14
Condemned with criminals	Isa. 53:12	Luke 23:32-33
Raging thirst when dying	Ps. 22:15	John 19:28-29
Crucified [hands and feet pierced]	Ps. 22:16	John 19:18
Side pierced	Isa. 53:5	John 19:34
Buried by a rich man	Isa. 53:9	Luke 23:50-53
Suffering not the end	Isa. 53:11	Luke 24:1-8

the fulfillment of the Bible's promises.

• Jesus affirmed the Old Testament. He emphatically said, "I tell you the truth, until heaven and earth disappear, not the smallest letter, not the least stroke of a pen, will by any means disappear from the Law until everything is accomplished" (Matt. 5:18). He quoted Scripture as final authority, often introducing a statement with the phrase, "It is written . . ." as in His encounter with Satan in the wilderness, when His demonic enemy tried to tempt Him (Matt. 4).

• Jesus spoke of Himself and of events surrounding His life as being fulfillments of Scripture: "But this has all taken place that the writings of the prophets might be fulfilled" (Matt. 26:56).

When Jesus first started teaching, He sat in the synagogue in Nazareth, where He grew up. An attendant handed Him a scroll containing the words of the Prophet Isaiah. Jesus unrolled the scroll and began to read the 800-year-old document. He read Isaiah 61:1-2, gave it back to the attendant, and sat down. Every eye was fixed on Him, intent on His next words, which were "Today this scripture is fulfilled in your hearing" (Luke 4:21).

Imagine the electricity when Jesus declared that He had fulfilled a prophecy written 800 years previously. Luke records, "All . . . were amazed at the gracious words that came from his lips" (v. 22). The watching crowd wanted Him to do miracles for them. Yet they felt a restraining reverence for Him as He read these words:

> The Spirit of the Lord is on me,
> because he has anointed me
> to preach good news to the poor.
> He has sent me to proclaim freedom for the prisoners
> and recovery of sight for the blind,
> to release the oppressed,
> to proclaim the year of the Lord's favor. (Luke 4:18-19)

• Perhaps Jesus' most sweeping endorsement and acceptance of the Old Testament was when He declared with finality, "The Scripture cannot be broken" (John 10:35).

If, then, we acknowledge Jesus Christ as Savior and Lord, it would be a contradiction and strangely inconsistent if we rejected the Scripture as the Word of God. This would find us in disagreement with the One whom we acknowledge to be the eternal God, the Creator of the universe.

• Some have suggested that Jesus only *appeared* to accept the Old Testament and that He accommodated Himself to the prejudices of His contemporary hearers. In other words, He went along with His culture's view on the Scriptures and other issues. The theory is, because the teachers in the synagogue accepted the Old Testament as authoritative, He appealed to it to gain wider acceptance for His own teaching.

As the Nazareth incident shows, however, grave difficulties beset this thesis. Jesus' recognition and use of the authority of the Old Testament was not superficial or peripheral. It continued to be the heart of His teaching concerning His person and work. Otherwise, Jesus would be guilty of grave deception in His teaching. Moreover, why would He accommodate Himself on some points and not on others? This is doubtless an untenable position.

Helpful Definitions

Several definitions can illumine our understanding of the Bible as the Word of God.

1. *Accepting the Bible as the Word of God is not the same as regarding the entire Bible to be literal.* The question, Do you believe the Bible literally? is like the question, Have you stopped beating your wife? Either a yes or a no convicts the one who responds. When the question is asked about the Bible, the term *literal* needs to be carefully defined.

A "literal view" of the Bible does not mean that we do not recognize figures of speech used in Scripture. When Isaiah said "the trees of the field will clap their hands" (Isa. 55:12), and the psalmist said "mountains skipped like rams" (Ps. 114:4), no rational reading of these metaphorical descriptions would view them in literal terms. Biblical writers used poetry, prose, and other literary forms. A literal view interprets any passage in the sense the authors intended. This is the same principle one employs when reading the newspaper, where it is remarkably easy to distinguish between figures of speech and those statements a writer intends his or her readers to take literally—especially on the sports pages!

On the other hand, if we do not take those passages of the Bible literally that God intended to be literal, we can easily miss or change the obvious intent of the authors. Such a view would interpret certain biblical events (for instance, the initial sin of humanity beginning with Adam and Eve) as nonfactual stories recorded to illustrate and convey only spiritual truth.

Those holding this view would like to allegorize any part of the Bible by saying it is similar to our reading Aesop's fables. "Don't kill the goose that lays the golden egg" is an application. Its truth does not hinge on the literal existence of a goose or a golden egg. Certainly the fable was meant to be read this way. In the same manner, this view of the Bible would feel free to allegorize any of the historical, biblical events. The result would be a completely subjective interpretation of the truth conveyed by God's Word.

Put simply, this logic bypasses the grammatical and syntactic intent of the words. It would even miss the overall unity of God's covenant, which is to deliver "all the world" and fulfilling it literally in Jesus Christ. Biblical events such as the cross and the resurrection of Jesus Christ would be seen as legends conveying no vital importance. The avoidance of "literal" could lead to a pick-and-choose interpretation removing any thought of divine biblical inspiration. The expression "taking the Bible literally," therefore, is ambiguous and requires careful definition.

2. *The phrase "the Bible is inerrant" also must be defined.* What does this rather difficult term *inerrancy* mean and what does it not mean? In brief, here is a general definition: "In the original manuscripts, the thoughts that God wanted written were written. In addition, God guarded the words the biblical writers used."

• Twentieth-century standards for scientific and historical precision do not hold true for *any* ancient writings. The Scripture describes things "phenomenologically," as things appear to be, even as things appear to us. It speaks of the sun rising and

> # God's revelation is designed to make us Christians, not scientists!
>
> • He made everything.
> • He made everything out of nothing.
> • He made everything good.

setting. We know that the sun doesn't actually rise and set but that the earth rotates. We use sunrise and sunset, even in an age of scientific enlightenment. This is a convenient way of describing *what appears to be*. Consequently, we cannot charge the Bible with error when it speaks phenomenologically. It speaks in this way, as have people of all ages and cultures.

• The same standards of exactness in historical matters were not used in ancient times. Although illustrations abound of the ways in which biblical writers recorded wars, dynasties, and reigns of kings with verifiable accuracy, they also used round numbers rather than precise figures. Incidentally, we frequently round numbers as well. In fact, when the police estimate the number in a large crowd, the figure is not precise, but it is close enough for their purpose.

• Some apparent errors may be errors in transcription when hand copying the texts. This, of course, was their only way of duplicating copies throughout the centuries. Gutenberg invented the printing press and printed the first Bible in the 1450s. Although tedious, hand copying produced thousands of copies. Nevertheless, evidence is replete with countless examples of transcribers demonstrating incredible accuracy and utmost care to each copy, showing remarkably few variations from text to text.

In comparing the existing thousands of biblical documents, some problems as yet do not yield a ready explanation. We can freely admit this, remembering many times in the past, possible discrepancies in a text were resolved when more data became available. The logical position, then, would be where there are areas of seeming contradictions to hold the problem in abeyance. We can admit our present inability to explain and await the possibility of new data. The presence of problems does not prevent us from accepting the Bible as the supernatural Word of God, however, because those discrepancies have minor bearing on the central teachings of Jesus Christ.

E.J. Carnell puts it succinctly:

There is a close parallel between science and Christianity which surprisingly few seem to notice. As Christianity *assumes* that all in the Bible is supernatural, so the scientist *assumes* that all in nature is rational and orderly. Both are hypotheses based, not on all of the evidence, but on the evidence "for the most part." Science devoutly holds to the hypothesis that all of nature is mechanical, though, as a matter of fact, the mysterious electron keeps jumping around as expressed by what is called *the Heisenberg principle of uncertainty*.

How does science justify its hypothesis that all of nature is mechanical, when it admits on other grounds many areas of nature do not seem to conform to this pattern? The answer is that since regularity is observed in nature "for the most part," the smoothest hypothesis is to assume that it is the same throughout the whole.[5]

Astonishing Prophecies

A further indication that the Bible is the Word of God is in the remarkable number of fulfilled prophecies it contains.

These prophecies are not vague generalities like those given by modern fortune-tellers: "A handsome man/woman will soon come into your life." Such predictions are susceptible to easy misinterpretation. Many Bible prophecies are specific in their details, and the authentication and veracity of the prophet rests on them. The Scripture itself makes it clear that fulfilled prophecy is one of the evidences of the supernatural origin of the words of its prophets (Jer. 28:9).

The writer of the Book of Deuteronomy tells us that failure of fulfillment of a prophecy unmasks a false prophet: "You may say to yourselves, 'How can we know when a message has not been spoken by the Lord?' If what a prophet proclaims in the name of the Lord does not take place or come true, that is a message the Lord has not spoken. That prophet has spoken presumptuously. Do not be afraid of him" (Deut. 18:21-22).

Isaiah also ties the unmasking of false prophets to the failure of their predictive prophecy. "Bring in your idols to tell us what is going to happen. Tell us what the former things were, so that we may consider them and know their final outcome. Or declare to us the things to come, tell us what the future holds, so we may know that you are gods. Do something, whether good or bad, so that we will be dismayed and filled with fear" (Isa. 41:22-23).

Three kinds of prophecies are seen in the Old Testament:

• *There are predictions of a coming Messiah, the Lord Jesus Christ—some in precise detail.* The early disciples quoted the Old Testament prophecies regularly, proclaiming that Jesus was the fulfillment of these prophecies.

Many of these were written by prophets 500 to 1,000 years before Christ came to earth. This kind of specific detail is unequaled in any other major religion of the world.

We can mention only a small but representative number of the prophecies. Jesus referred to the predictive prophecies about Himself in what must have been one of the most exciting Bible studies in history. After conversation with two disciples on the road to Emmaus, Jesus said, " 'How slow of heart to believe all that the prophets have spoken! Did not the Christ have to suffer these things and then enter his glory?' And beginning with Moses and all the Prophets, he explained to them what was said in all the Scriptures concerning himself" (Luke 24:25-27).

Isaiah 52:13–53:12 is the most outstanding example of predictive prophecy about Christ. Its contingencies could not have been rigged in advance in an attempt to produce fulfillment. Fifteen specific words or phrases can be found in these verses that fit Jesus' life exactly. They involve His life and the rejection of His ministry; His reactions to the unjust judicial proceedings prior to His crucifixion; His death, and finally His burial. These were written 800 years before Jesus lived!

The New Testament contains thirty-eight references to Isaiah 53 and twenty-four references to Psalm 22.[6]

Micah 5:2 is a striking illustration of both a prediction about Christ and historical detail: "But you, Bethlehem Ephrathah, though you are small among the clans of Judah, out of you will come for me one who will be ruler over Israel, whose origins are from of old, from ancient times."

It took a decree from the mighty Caesar Augustus himself to have a census taken and bring Mary and Joseph from Nazareth to Bethlehem Ephrathah, where Jesus was born. The designation of Ephrathah was given because there was a second Bethlehem north of this one, which was not where Jesus was born. The Scripture was fulfilled exactly!

• *There are predictions that deal with kings, nations, and cities.* A most remarkable prediction has to do with the city of Tyre in Ezekiel 26. Here a whole series of little details are given as to how Tyre would be destroyed, the utter completeness of its destruction, and the fact that it would never be reconstructed (v. 4). How this prophecy was fulfilled by degrees in Nebuchadnezzar's attack and then through the savage onslaught of Alexander the Great is a phenomenal illustration of the accurateness and reality of predictive prophecy in the Bible. This is also only one of a number of such predictions.

• *There are predictions about the Jewish people, the Israelites.* Again, only a few of these startling prophecies will be cited.

Both Moses and the Prophet Hosea predicted that conquering nations would disperse the Jews from their homeland. "The Lord will cause you to be defeated before your enemies. You will come at them from one direction but flee from them in seven, and you will become a thing of horror to all the kingdoms on earth" (Deut. 28:25). "Because they have not obeyed him; they will be wanderers among the nations" (Hosea 9:17).

Remarkably the Prophet Jeremiah made the astonishing prediction of the restoration of Israel as a nation (Jer. 31). For centuries, this was considered to be unthinkable. Some events in our own time, however, may well be at least partial fulfillment of these prophecies. All observers agree that the reestablishment of Israel as a nation in 1948 is one of the amazing political phenomena of our day.

One cannot deny the force of fulfilled prophecy as evidence of divine guidance. Furthermore, these are prophecies that could not possibly have been schemed and written after the events were predicted.

God Speaks through This Book

There are, then, a number of pieces of evidence on which one can reasonably base his or her belief that the Bible is the Word of God. As one reads the Bible, the confirmation of its truth is what finally turns doubt into belief. As a person views the evidence and reads the Bible, "it dawns on him," to use Gordon Clark's phrase, that the Bible is the Word of God.[7] This realization begins with seeing how God speaks and is concerned for each of us. His words are never trivial but always toward some purpose. As one reads, the mind is enlightened, the heart is touched, and there comes a convincing discernment of the Scripture's message.

The two disciples on the road to Emmaus asked, "Were not our hearts burning within us?" (Luke 24:32) This same experience becomes ours as we continue to open ourselves to the possibility of the Divine Author Himself speaking to us. He has taken the initiative!

Are the Bible Documents Reliable?

Several years ago a national magazine featured an article that
claimed that there are thousands of errors in the Bible. In response
to such claims, we should ask, How do we know that the text of the
Bible as we have it today, having come to us through many translations
and versions over the centuries, is not just a pale reflection of the original? What guarantee do we have that deletions and embellishments have
not obscured the original message of the Bible? What difference does the
historical accuracy of the Bible make? Surely the only thing that counts
is the message!

Christians, however, believe Christianity is rooted in history. For
example, Jesus Christ was counted in a Roman census. Yet, if the Bible's
historical references are not true, grave questions may be raised about it.
In addition, are the "spiritual" parts of its message true, encased as they
are in historical events? Are the books now included in the Bible substantially the same documents the people had almost 2,000 years ago?
How do we know whether other books should have been included?

These questions and others are worthy of answers.

In finding answers to this litany of questions, let us first remind ourselves of the primary truths we have established from the previous chapters.

- There is a rational body of truth for belief in God and in Jesus Christ. No need to kiss our brains good-bye.
- God exists and is personal and knowable. He desires to communicate with us, His creation.
- God has come to earth in the incarnation of Jesus Christ to establish a personal and intimate relationship with us.
- God has used the medium of words—the Bible—to reveal Himself, His character, and His plan to us.

At this point we must examine the Bible for its credentials and reliability. God's Word describes events covering many generations, and He used about forty authors to write the texts of His Word. The accuracy and truthfulness of these accounts is of paramount importance, and the process of establishing the accuracy is no small task. Examining the origins of the sixty-six books contained in Scripture is called the science of textual criticism. It has to do with the reliability of the text—that is, how our current text compares with the original documents and how accurately the ancient manuscripts were copied.

Before the Printing Press

The ancient manuscripts, of course, had no pages as we have now. For the preservation of the Old Testament (or the Hebrew Bible), priests and scribes used clay and wooden tablets, as well as reed papyrus and parchment skins, which were rolled into scrolls. In addition, archaeologists have uncovered pottery pieces and even beaten metal fragments on which were written Scripture. Evidently the ancient writing instrument was either an iron stylus or a reed pen sharpened with a penknife. Because not everyone could read or had a scroll, a high premium was placed on the public reading and hearing of these documents. This helps us understand the emphasis placed on the phrase "hearing the word of the Lord" in the Old Testament.[1]

It wasn't until about A.D. 1456 that Gutenberg created the first moveable type printing press and printed his first book, the Bible in Latin.

From then on, both the availability of books and the habit of reading increased dramatically.

The work of the "scribes" or "copyists" with the scrolls was a highly professional and carefully executed task in ancient times. For the Hebrews, devout Jews with the highest dedication undertook this task. Because they believed they were dealing with the Word of God, they were acutely aware of the need for extreme care and accuracy. Their devotion is seen in habits like wiping a pen clean before writing the name of God and counting the letters of both the original and the one copied. In some cases, when discrepancies were found, the entire copy was destroyed.

The earliest and most widely used copy of the entire Hebrew Bible is from around A.D. 900. This is called the Masoretic text, being the product of able Jewish scribes, who were known as the Masoretes (literally "transmitters") and were custodians of the Hebrew text from A.D. 500 to 1000. The Hebrew text of the Old Testament used today is called the Masoretic text, validating the quality of a work done more than a thousand years ago. All of the present copies of the Hebrew text we have today are in remarkable agreement with this text. Copying and proofreading was indeed a skillful art. Furthermore, confirmation of the accuracy of a text is checked by comparing it with the Latin and Greek copies from the same time period.

The Dead Sea Scrolls

In 1947 the world learned about what has been called the greatest archaeological discovery of the century. In caves in the valley of the Dead Sea, ancient jars were discovered containing the now-famous Dead Sea Scrolls. From these scrolls, it is evident that a group of dedicated Jews lived at a place near the Dead Sea called Qumran from about 150 B.C. to A.D. 70.

Qumran was a communal society, operated much like a monastery. In addition to tilling the fields, they spent their time studying and copying the Hebrew Scriptures. In A.D. 70 it became apparent to them that the Romans were going to devastate the Jewish people, along with their religious culture. Therefore, they put their leather scrolls into jars and hid the jars in caves in the side of the cliffs west of the Dead Sea.

In the providence of God the scrolls survived undisturbed until a young Bedouin goat herdsman accidentally found them in February or

March of 1947. After a careful exploration of the area, archaeologists discovered eleven other caves containing scrolls. The find included the earliest manuscript copy yet known of the complete Book of Isaiah, and another one containing about one-third of the book. Later discoveries yielded *fragments of every book in the Old Testament* except the Book of Esther.

In addition, there is a fragmented copy containing much of Isaiah chapters 38 to 66. The Books of Samuel, in a tattered copy, were also found at that time, along with two complete chapters of Habakkuk. A number of nonbiblical items, including the rules for the ancient community, were uncovered as well.

Because of those who question the accuracy of the Old Testament text, we can easily see the significance of this find. In one dramatic stroke, almost 1,000 years were bridged closing the gap in the age of the manuscripts we now possess. It might be similar to being told a painting you owned is not 200 years old, but a thousand years old. Comparing the Dead Sea Scrolls with the Masoretic text has resulted in the proof that remarkable accuracy occurred in the transmission process. Thus a period of nearly a millennium was closed.

What was actually learned? Comparison between the Qumran manuscript of Isaiah (chapters 38–66) with the one we had before gives an exciting picture. Scholars found:

The text is extremely close to our Masoretic text. A comparison of Isaiah 53 shows that only seventeen letters differ from the Masoretic text. Ten of these are mere differences of spelling, like our "honor" or "honour" and produce no change in the meaning at all. Four others are extremely minor differences, such as the presence of the conjunction, which is often a matter of style. The other

BENEFITS FROM THE SCROLLS

• They confirmed the accuracy of 1,000 years of both the recording and the history of the Hebrews—that is, from 200 B.C. to A.D. 916.

• The scrolls' translation and the official text used in the Jerusalem Temple reinforce each other's accuracy above all other manuscripts.

• The extensive evidence found strengthens our confidence in the histories previously uncovered. As a result, earlier copies of the Pentateuch and histories also have a high probability of accuracy.

three letters are the Hebrew word for "light," which is added after "they shall see" in verse 11. Out of 166 words in this chapter, only this one word is really in question, and it does not at all change the sense of the passage. This is typical of the whole manuscript.[2]

Three Important Versions

Because the Hebrew people migrated throughout eastern Asia due to travel and wars, other scrolls have been found from Egypt to Rome. Comparing these with one another has fortified our confidence in the historicity of earlier events described in the Old Testament.

• *The Septuagint*, meaning seventy, is a Greek translation of the Old Testament and is the oldest and most important. While the presence of the Jewish people was evident throughout the Middle East, the great Greek empire under Alexander the Great hellenized the region in about 250 B.C. Consequently, many Jewish people knew no Hebrew, only Greek, and failed to participate in the temple worship. Referred to as the LXX and translated by seventy-two Jewish scholars in the third and second centuries B.C., this Greek translation became a bridge for understanding the Hebrew history and theology in the Old Testament.

• *The Syriac version* written in the Aramaic language of Syria is the oldest and most important translation after the Septuagint. It continued in use with some revisions from the Septuagint.

• *The Samaritan version* is another ancient account similar to the others. This one contains copies of the Hebrew Pentateuch. Unquestionably it is derived from the split between the Jerusalem Jews and the Samaritans. Copies of the old scrolls of the Pentateuch are extant today in Nablus (Shechem), Palestine.

These and other types of texts existed in 200 B.C. We can conclude with R. Laird Harris:

We can now be sure that copyists worked with great care and accuracy on the Old Testament, even back to 225 B.C. Although some differed among themselves, it was so little, we can infer that still earlier copyists had also faithfully and carefully transmitted the Old

Testament text. Indeed, it would be rash skepticism that would now deny that we have our Old Testament in a form very close to that used by Ezra when he taught the Law to those who had returned from the Babylonian captivity—about 457 B.C. (Ezra 9–10).[3]

New Testament Documents

Not more than one-thousandth part of the whole New Testament is affected by differences of reading. This was the conclusion of the great scholar F.J.A. Hort from a lifetime of studying early documentary evidence. He added there are only insignificant variations in grammar or spelling between various documents in the New Testament.[4]

Originally written in Greek, the latest number of manuscripts now known tops 5,500; some are complete and some are very small fragments. One of these fragments, determined to be the very earliest of all, comes from John 18 and has only five verses—three on one side and two on the other—about the size of a 3 x 5 card. Because this fragment came from Egypt and was copied and circulated from Patmos, Asia Minor, where the Apostle John was exiled, a group of scholars estimated it must have been composed (at least) by A.D. 90–100.[5]

Unlike the Old Testament, writing was done with ink and pen, mostly on papyrus (from the plant) or parchment (animal skin). References are made to the ink in 2 John 12 and 3 John 13. In addition, the Apostle Paul made a poignant request in a letter to his friends to bring him a cloak he had left behind "and my scrolls, especially the parchments." It is assumed the parchments he mentioned were the Old Testament on animal skin (2 Tim. 4:13).

The flood of documentary evidence brings us to the point where we need to ask when the New Testament was written. It is generally agreed that the crucifixion of Jesus Christ took place about A.D. 30. According to the New Testament scholar F.F. Bruce, this event has been carefully compared with the dates of the ruling emperor, Tiberius Caesar, as well as with other Roman hierarchy. The New Testament was complete or substantially complete by about A.D. 100, and the majority of the writing was accomplished long before this time by contemporaries of Christ. These writers were still alive; they saw, heard, and remembered things Jesus had done and said.[6]

The time that elapsed between the actual events and the writing of the books, from the standpoint of historical research, is actually short. Some of the Pauline letters are even earlier than some of the Gospels.

Again, based on the evidence, the text we read today does not differ in any substantial way from the originals as it came from the hands of the human writers.[7]

The extraordinary number of copies of early New Testament materials defies imagination. When we compare it with other documents of ancient writings from the same time, it fills us with admiration. For the New Testament there are two excellent manuscripts from the fourth century A.D., and fragments of papyrus copies of books of the New Testament date from 100 to 200 years earlier still.[8]

By contrast, among the works of classical writers, contemporaries of Christ, no one questions the existence of these secular authors or the validity of their writings. Have you ever heard anyone ask, "How do we know Socrates ever lived?" (about 400 B.C.). Yet there is far less supportive documentary evidence for his existence and the lives of other contemporary Greek and Latin writers than there is for Jesus Christ. The

DATES AND NUMBER OF MANUSCRIPTS BY SECULAR WRITERS		
Writer/Earliest Know Manuscript	Date of Writer	Number of Manuscripts
Thucycides/1,300 yrs after he lived	460–400 B.C.	8
Aristotle (*Poetics*) 1,400 yrs after he lived	343 B.C.	5
Caesar (*Gallic Wars*) 900 yrs after he lived	58–50 B.C.	9–10

DATES AND NUMBER OF NEW TESTAMENT DOCUMENTS		
Paul, James Gospel Writers/70 yrs after they lived	A.D. 40–60 A.D. 60–100	5,500 + (in all)

four Gospels, twenty-one letters, the history of Acts, and the visions of Revelation have a manuscript attestation second to none. On the preceding page is a chart of comparative numbers and dates.[9]

Additional Confirmation

Other sources support the authenticity of the New Testament, particularly as the church spread. In fact, both friends and enemies of Christianity used references and quotations from the New Testament books. The early church fathers, writing mostly between A.D. 90 and 160, give indication of familiarity

> **"The Word of God is like a lion. You don't have to defend a lion. All you have to do is let the lion loose, and the lion will defend itself."**
>
> *Charles Spurgeon*

with most of the books of the New Testament. Even the Gnostic school of Valentinus (those searching for salvation through knowledge) was also familiar with most of the New Testament.[10]

• *Versions* are those manuscripts translated from the Greek into other languages. In addition to the Syriac versions, there are the Egyptian or Coptic versions and Latin versions. Fragments of papyrus copies of books of the New Testament date from the fourth century A.D. and earlier. By careful study of these versions, important clues have been uncovered as to the original Greek manuscripts from which they were translated.

• *Lectionaries*, the reading lessons used in public church services, are another source. More than 1,800 of these reading lessons have been classified. There are lectionaries of the Gospels, the Acts of the Apostles, and the Epistles. Though they did not appear before the sixth century, the text from which they quoted are generally early and of high quality. Though there have been many changes in the many copies of the New Testament writings, most of them are minor. The trustworthiness of our New Testament text deserves our informed respect.

When we are confronted with published accounts of biblical "errors," we can rest with the conclusion of the late Sir Frederic Kenyon, a world-renowned scholar of the ancient manuscripts. He said, "The interval, then, between the dates of original composition and the earliest extant evidence becomes so small as to be in fact negligible, and the last foundation for any doubt that the Scriptures have come down to us substantially as they were written has now been removed. Both the authenticity and the general integrity of the books of the New Testament may be regarded as finally established."[11]

The Question of the Canon

A question closely allied to that of the reliability of the texts we have is, How do we know the books in our Bible, and no others, are the ones that should be there? This is called the question of the canon—the list of books seen as inspired by God. There are distinct questions involved for the Old and New Testaments.

The thirty-nine books of the Hebrew Bible are divided into three groups:
• *The Law:* The first five books of the Bible, Genesis to Deuteronomy; they are also called the Torah or Pentateuch
• *The Prophets:*
"Former Prophets": Joshua, Judges, 1–2 Samuel, 1–2 Kings
"Latter Prophets": Isaiah, Jeremiah, and Ezekiel
"The Book of the Twelve": those prophets from Hosea to Malachi
• *The Writings:* the remaining books of the Old Testament canon—Ruth, 1–2 Chronicles, Ezra, Nehemiah, Esther, Job, Psalms, Proverbs, Song of Solomon, Ecclesiastes, Lamentations, Daniel

The Protestant version of the Old Testament is similar to the Hebrew Bible of the Jewish people. Meanwhile, since the Council of Trent in 1546, the Roman Catholic Church also includes the books of the Apocrypha. The order in the English Bible follows that of the Septuagint.

Believers have received these sacred books as authoritative because they believe that God inspired the authors of the Bible in order to reveal His holy Word. E.J. Young comments:

When the Word of God was written, it became Scripture, and as it had been spoken by God, it possessed His absolute 'authority. Therefore, it was the Word of God and was canonical. That which determines the canonicity of a book, therefore, is the fact that the book is inspired of God.[12]

We can see this development first in the work of Moses, who issued God's laws governing the Jewish people. Later the ancient Israelites regarded the words of the Hebrew prophets as decrees from God Himself. This belief continued with succeeding generations. Although the nation of Israel neglected the Mosaic Law at times, the spiritual leaders among the Jews recognized its authority. This profound recognition shook King Josiah when he realized how long the Law had been neglected: "When the king heard the words of the Book of the Law, he tore his robes" (2 Kings 22:11).

By the beginning of the Christian era, the term *Scripture* had come to mean a fixed body of divinely inspired writings, which were fully recognized as authoritative. It is interesting that there was no controversy between Jesus and the Pharisees regarding the authority of the Old Testament. Contention arose because the Pharisees placed tradition on the same level with the authority of Scripture. To some degree, we still today need to be aware when tradition rears its head for controversy. Indeed, we should always differentiate between truth and tradition when we are establishing the basis for our faith.

The church Council of Jamnia held informal discussions about the canon in A.D. 90. Whether any formal or binding decisions were made is problematic. However, there was a firm confirmation at a church council in Carthage in A.D. 397 when the New Testament canon was fixed.

The Apocryphal Books

The Apocryphal (meaning "hidden") books were twelve books never received into the Jewish canon. They were not considered as part of the inspired Scriptures by Jews or Christians in the early centuries of the Christian era. This is evident from a study of the writings of Josephus, the Jewish historian, and of Augustine, the great North African bishop of Hippo. It is noteworthy that the New Testament writers do not once quote the Apocrypha.

The Apocryphal books themselves do not claim to be the Word of God or the work of the prophets. They vary greatly in content and value, giving some helpful historical background. Though not included at first, these books were later added to the Septuagint, and then the church father Jerome included them in the Latin Vulgate in the early fifth century. Jerome, however, did not regard the Apocryphal books as part of the canon. Much later, in the sixteenth century, the Catholic church elevated the Apocrypha to canonical status at the Council of Trent.

For the Old Testament we have, ultimately, the witness of Jesus to the canonicity of the thirty-nine books we now have.

The New Testament Canon

The twenty-nine books in the New Testament were received as part of the canon by virtue of their inspiration, not by vote. Much of the material of the New Testament claimed apostolic authority. Peter and Paul clearly wrote with this authority in mind. In fact, Peter specifically referred to Paul's letters as Scripture (2 Peter 3:1-16).

Jude (v. 18) says that 2 Peter 3:3 is a word from the apostles. Such early church fathers as Polycarp, Ignatius, and Clement mentioned a number of the New Testament books as authoritative.

The final fixation of the canon as we know it today came in the fourth century. In a letter by Athanasius in A.D. 367, he distinguished between works in the canon, which are described as the sole sources of religious instruction, and other books, which believers were permitted to read. In the same year, a decision at a church council held at Carthage fixed the final canon.

Three criteria were generally used throughout this period of time to establish whether the particular written documents were the true record of the voice and message of apostolic witness.

- *Was the book authored by an apostle?* The Gospels of Mark and Luke do not meet this criterion specifically, but were accepted as the works of close associates of the apostles.
- *Was the book widely recognized by the church?* This centered on the matter of ecclesiastical usage. A canonical book had to be broadly accepted by the churches.
- *Was the teaching of the book in conformity to standards of sound doctrine preached in the churches?*

These data are helpful and interesting, but in the final analysis, as with the question of the inspiration of the Scripture, canonicity is a question of the witness of God to each individual, confirming the truth in the hearts of those who read it.

In days of uncertainty, the Scriptures and character of the One who inspired them give us a firm rock on which to stand, intellectually and spiritually! "Heaven and earth will pass away," declared our Lord, "but my words will never pass away" (Luke 21:33).

Does Archaeology Verify Scripture?

I n the early years of the nineteenth century, a new door of information opened to uncover the earliest roots of the human race in the Near East. Increased travel and exploration provided the hinges to the door, and modern archaeologists walked through with a spurt of enthusiasm. They began to dig below the earth's surface for the material remains of humankind's past found in ancient palaces, buried temples, and animal stables.

Civilizations came alive that existed long before the known world of Greece and Rome. Babylon (called "great"), where Daniel lived, revealed double walls with nine ornamented gates. Egypt showed marvels of painted tombs, bandaged mummies, mirrors, perfume jars, and mascara pots.

At first the buried cultures themselves were the objects of study. Then there appeared places and names from the Old Testament on the palace walls. Names of Assyrian tyrants who warred with Israel, along with their armies and hapless captives, were found. Persian governors spoke through their letters. The pharaohs of Egypt, some lying in solid gold coffins, could now be identified.

In the wake of these discoveries, biblical scholars have found rich background for the biblical history of Israel and her neighbors. The historical and geographical reliability of the Bible was affirmed in a number of important areas. This was in marked contrast to previous centuries when there was little evidence to corroborate the Bible's historical statements. Critics then would dismiss the narratives by casting them as implausible stories set in fictional backgrounds rather than as historical events. But by the middle of the twentieth century it was recognized that archaeological discoveries were substantiating the biblical record. In fact, well-known secular scholars affirmed this new attitude toward the historical reliability of the Bible with enlightening statements.

"There can be no doubt that archeology has confirmed the substantial historicity of Old Testament tradition," states Dr. W.F. Albright of Johns Hopkins University.[1] Dr. Millar Burrows, a professor at Yale University, adds,

On the whole . . . archaeological work has unquestionably strengthened confidence in the reliability of the scriptural record. More than one archaeologist has found his respect for the Bible increased by the experience of excavation in Palestine. Archaeology has in many cases refuted the views of modern critics. It has shown, in a number of instances, that these views rest on false assumptions and unreal, artificial schemes of historical development. This is a real contribution and not to be minimized.[2]

Biblical History Confirmed

The help from archaeology covers several categories.

• It has verified some specific biblical events previously doubted and even ridiculed. The impact of this skepticism is shown in the observation of one scholar that it is a rare biblical passage that someone has not questioned.

• In addition, archaeology's help has been more general in nature, filling in the overall background of the culture and practices of biblical times. Such things as economic problems and literary development describe the world to which the Old Testament prophets spoke.

• Some points of apparent conflict between the biblical record and the information previously available have been surprisingly cleared up as more information has been obtained. It would seem, therefore, that when apparent conflicts still exist, rather than conclude that the Bible must be wrong, a more reasonable position would be to admit the problem exists and to hold it open pending further discoveries.

Having said all this, however, our point of reference is always that we cannot prove the Bible by archaeology, nor do we *believe* the Bible on the basis of archaeological proof. H. Darrell Lance writes to this point: "Although archaeology can sometimes provide independent evidence for the existence of certain places, persons or events mentioned in the Bible, it can say nothing at all about whether God had anything to do with any of it. That, for the modern believer as well as for the ancient Israelite, is a matter of faith."[3]

In addition to faith, it is God who ultimately confirms the spiritual truth of Scripture as we read it. Archaeology confirms the accounts recorded. Spiritual truth comes from God Himself. The historical details repeatedly confirmed by archaeology inspire our confidence to look beyond the historical events to "The Story of God"—The Story with a capital S, as Leighton Ford expresses it.[4]

Sources of Archaeologists

More than 25,000 sites showing some connection with the Old Testament period have been located in the Bible lands. Yet there is still a wealth of material that awaits discovery. Throughout the Near East mounds of earth and debris (called "tells") mark the place where towns or cities once flourished. According to A.R. Millard, most of the major cities of the Bible can be identified either by "general geographical considerations or by tradition (though that may not be very reliable) or by current use of the ancient name."[5]

An excellent example of ancient

> **Archaeology confirms the biblical accounts in more than 25,000 sites connected to biblical history.**

names surviving to this day is the city of Damascus. Known to us through the Apostle Paul's conversion in Acts 9, Damascus has existed with that name for 3,500 years or more.

Ancient Eastern inscriptions from the entire Middle East give insightful support to data in the Bible. On stones, pottery, walls, and other places are writings in languages of countries neighboring ancient Israel. Pictures and other artifacts open up details of these cultures.

Excavation of biblical sites themselves expand the information related to the stories told. They tell us how people lived, how they built houses, and how they labored. Excavations have revealed the existence and amazing skills of whole civilizations. In fact, the correlation with biblical data is so vast that we can spotlight only a few major contributions.

How Are the Finds Dated?

Ancient cities were built, then disintegrated with time, and later rebuilt in the same place. Thus a succession of levels is commonly found at these sites, the lowest of course, being the oldest. The question arises, How can these finds be dated?

Fashions in pottery changed in each new culture. If a particular fashion at one excavated site can be dated, a similar pottery found elsewhere would obviously be from the same period. Kings often inscribed their names on the hinge-sockets of temple doors, and the names of their gods would be given. Furthermore, inscribed stones were often laid under palace or temple walls in memory of the founder. Royal sepulchers were identified in the same way.

Copies of lists of events and people have been uncovered dating back to almost 2000 B.C. Sumerian scribes drew up some of these lists, cataloging their kings according to their successive dynasties with notes as to the length of their reigns. A few miles from the city of Ur, the early home of Abraham, a foundation stone was uncovered. The stone had been laid by a king, whose name is unknown, of the First Dynasty of Ur. Significantly, the scribes speak of this as the third dynasty after the Flood. This king apparently reigned 3,100 years before Christ and more than a thousand years before Abraham.[6]

2000 B.C.—Abraham's Time

A good example of the help archaeology can be to us pertains to the life and times of Abraham (about 2166–1991 B.C.). The discovery of three cities—

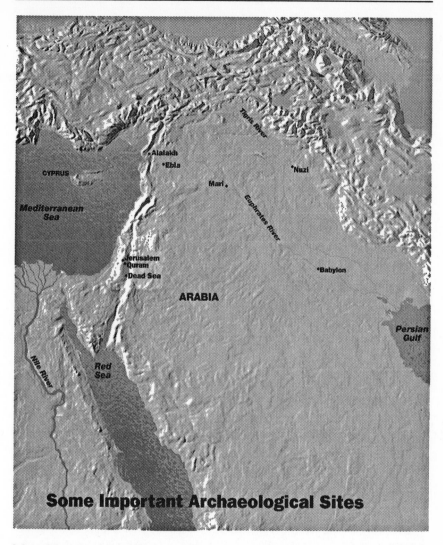

Some Important Archaeological Sites

Mari, Nuzi, and Alalakh—disclosed new information of ancient civilizations, giving clues of the life in Syria and Mesopotamia both historically
and politically. In addition, we get a new view into the pastoral lives of
the patriarchs Abraham, Isaac, and Jacob—the founding fathers of the
ancient Israelites.

These records cover a broad spectrum from business to politics, government, and the arts. They reflect customs and social relationships that
parallel the situations the biblical patriarchs faced. When we see
Abraham in the settings similar to those of the cities of Mari and Nuzi,
the biblical accounts become highly credible and believable. The life and

history, the political movements, and the cultural and business activities of these cities paint a wonderfully illuminated background of the world of the father of the Hebrew nation.

In 1933 a party of Arabs were digging a grave by the upper Euphrates River just ten miles from the Iraqi border. They unearthed a stone statue and then reported their find. Subsequently a team of archaeologists unearthed a city named Mari at this site. They dug out more statues and eventually unearthed an elaborate palace bearing the name of the city. This was not a small royal palace. It covered more than six acres and had more than 260 rooms, courtyards, and passages. A.R. Millard observes:

> Archaeologists usually concentrate on the more rewarding parts, where temples or palaces stood, or lay out their trenches to probe each period of existence in the life of the place. To do this a trench may slice right through the mound, producing a small amount of information at all levels.
>
> Any area of special interest can be marked and explored with a larger trench. Each building or time of occupation will have left its mark on the mound in the form of floor surfaces, stumps of walls, and heaps of rubbish. These will be sandwiched between earlier remains below and later remains above.[7]

Millard describes the palace as containing rooms with walls fifteen feet high, some empty and some filled with jars that stood ready for oil, wine, or grain. There were spacious living quarters for the king, his wives, and his family; and more cramped ones for officials and servants. One can imagine craftsmen in workshops, cooks in the kitchens, secretaries, servants, and singing troupes for the king's entertainment. One of the many statues found was of a bearded man dating from the eighteenth century B.C. and inscribed with the name Ishtupilum, King of Mari.[8]

Some 20,000 cuneiform (wedge-shaped writing) tablets from royal archives were found. Accountants had used some of the tablets to record grain, vegetables, and other provisions brought into the palace. Letters to the king, musical instruments, and gold for decorations are also mentioned. There are even letters with messages from prophets to gods. A jar of buried treasure and inscriptions date the city around 2500 B.C.

The collection of tablets is the largest known in the literature of the ancient Middle East containing prophecies comparable to the kinds written by Israel's prophets at the time. Since Abraham is variously thought to have lived during the same general era between the nineteenth and twentieth centuries B.C., this is certainly the kind of culture in which he lived.

Another city, Nuzi, situated east of the city of Mari near the Tigris River, produced tablets detailing some of the social customs of the city in the fourteenth and fifteenth centuries B.C. Families are described in situations similar to the dilemma Abraham faced in Genesis 15:4 when Sarah, his wife, accepted Ishmael as her own son. According to that custom, if the couple later had a natural child, the adopted son would have to yield some of his rights to the second son. In the case of Abraham and Sarah, Isaac, Sarah's natural son, received the entire inheritance of his parents, and Ishmael was banished.

The Nuzi tablets tell a story similar to the incident in Genesis 16:1-2 in which Sarah presented her Egyptian handmaid, Hagar, to Abraham in order to bear a child because she had been unable to conceive. Bible scholar Edwin M. Yamauchi tells us of a "tablet of adoption which stipulated that a barren wife must provide a slave girl to her husband to beget a son. This particular tablet and the Hammurabi Law Code requires that the slave's child be kept—a rule which was preempted by the divine command to send Hagar and Ishmael away."[9]

Another Syrian site, Alalakh on the Orontes River, yielded an artifact, which describes wife abuse. A husband who mistreated a wife (literally "drags her by the nose") had to give up his wife and her dowry, and the right to the bridal gift presented to her family at the time of their marriage.[10]

Writing in the Third Millenium B.C.

Did you ever wonder about the literary abilities of the scribes during the time of the patriarchs? The bustling city of Ebla provides the largest early archive thus far unearthed from the Near East. It dates back to the third millennium B.C. Although Ebla's existence had been known, its location and highly developed culture was uncertain. Archaeologists have determined that the city was divided into two sectors, an acropolis and a lower city. The upper division contained four building complexes, including the palace of the king, a temple to the goddess Ishtar, and numerous stables. The lower section was divided into four quarters boasting four gates.

In a room adjacent to the temple, archaeologists discovered an astonishing collection of thousands of tablets stacked on the floor. The small room had been burned. In the heat of the flames the brickwork was baked, and the tablets as well. As a result both room and tablets withstood the ravages of the centuries until they were uncovered in 1975. Thus history has been preserved for 5,000 years![11]

Years of research and translations will be required, but the tablets do provide valuable evidence that cuneiform writing had spread to northern Syria before 2300 B.C. It also shows the habit of recording every sort of activity—both business and cultural. Dictionaries confirm the presence of west Semitic people of other languages in that era. Biblical history, we now know, took place in a world where writing was well established.

Israel's Kings

Archaeology has given us colorful background information for the study of the biblical kings. Solomon's grandeur has been the target of special skepticism. His lavish wealth is described in 1 Kings 9–10 as including a royal navy built on the shore of the Red Sea even though there is no suitable harbor on the coastline of Palestine. His army had use of 1,400 chariots and 1,200 horses. His building projects were extensive, including fortification of the cities of Jerusalem, Hazor, Megiddo, and Gezer (9:15). Recent excavation at these last three cities have at least documented Solomon's building skills.

In 1960 the famed Israeli scholar Yigael Yadin, while excavating the city of Megiddo, had identified the layer of Solomon's time by comparing pottery types. Knowing that 1 Kings 9:15 grouped together the three cities of Megiddo, Hazor, and Gezer as being built by Solomon, he had a sudden inspiration. He recalled that the Megiddo Gate from Solomon's time had three chambers on each side. Could the other two cities be the same? He tells this exciting story of the dig at Hazor:

> Before proceeding further with the excavation of Hazor, we made tentative markings on the ground following our estimate of the plan of the gate on the basis of the Megiddo Gate. And then we told the laborers to go ahead and continue removing the debris. When they had finished, they looked at us with astonishment, as if we were magicians or fortune-tellers. For there, before us, was the gate whose outline we had marked, a replica of the Megiddo Gate. This proved not only that both gates had been built by Solomon but that both had followed a single master plan.[12]

Solomon's Gold

First Kings 10:21 adds information that Solomon possessed large stores of precious metals. The temple he built for the Lord, like the golden shrine of King Tutankhaman of Egypt, was a glory of gold as described in the latter half of 1 Kings 6. "Solomon covered the inside of the temple with pure gold, and he extended gold chains across the front of the inner sanctuary, which was overlaid with gold. So he overlaid the whole interior with gold" (vv. 21-22). The entire concept is breathtaking.

Although the exact site of Solomon's Temple has not been found, other discoveries showed that kings of surrounding nations of his time possessed technology and workmanship similar to the biblical account. Millard elaborates:

Extravagant as this may seem, a display of gold was a matter of pride for any powerful ruler (i.e., valuable plates are displayed at royal banquets today). National currency reserves were held in gold, not stored idly in bank vaults to be publicized merely as figures, but shown to the populace. When a stronger army attacked, the gold was stripped and handed over to the conquerors (cf. 2 Kings 18:16).

Assyrian, Babylonian, and Egyptian monarchs boast of the gold they donated to beautify temples in their own cities. Their inscriptions speak of walls "covered with gold like plaster," of doors and doorways carved in relief and plated with gold, of furniture and decorations sheathed in precious metal. One Assyrian king seized six decorative golden shields from a temple in Armenia, each weighing twelve times as much as each of the shields Solomon hung in his palace (1 Kings 10:1-17; cf. 14:26-27). Claims of pompous emperors may be treated as grossly inflated, but with these uses of gold that is not so. Small fragments of thin gold sheets have been found in Assyria and Babylonia, and in Egypt nail holes . . . for attaching the metal are visible in . . . stonework.[13]

At least one of the sources of Solomon's gold came from Ophir. First Kings 9:11, as well as other passages, describes Hiram, king of Tyre, as supplying Solomon "with all the cedar and pine and gold he wanted." And verse 28 tells of Hiram's men who "sailed to Ophir and brought back 420 talents of gold, which they delivered to King Solomon." Although this city's exact location still remains a mystery (with conjectures ranging from the Somali coast of Africa to India), its existence and assets have been independently attested. A potsherd from the mid-eighth century B.C. has been unearthed at a port north of Tel Aviv. It carried the clear notation of the contents marked by a local clerk saying, "Ophir gold for Beth-Horon: 30 shekels" (about 340 g., 12 oz.).[14]

One conclusion can be safely made: Solomon's golden temple was no mere invention of exaggerating scribes. It falls into the known patterns of ancient practices of his times.

Israel and Moab's Conflict on Stone!

Some of the objects unearthed by archaeologists give specific details of biblical events. One example of this is a stone memorial telling of a conflict between Moab and Israel in 2 Kings 3:4ff. The Bible notes that Mesha, the king of Moab, and his people rebelled against Israel's rule over them and refused to pay tribute. A battle raged between Moab and the three kings of Israel, Judah, and Edom. The Moabites won the battle, and Israel abandoned its rule of over them.

In an 1868 excavation a German named Klein found an inscribed stone at Dibon, the land of Moab. Since Arabs living in Dibon owned the stone, he returned home to raise money for its purchase. Thinking they could get a higher price for it, the Arabs roasted the stone and then threw cold water over it to break it into pieces. Fortunately, Klein had taken an impression of the intact stone. Thus he was able to restore the fragments and translate them after its purchase. It is now at the Louvre in Paris. In an early form of the Phoenician alphabet (from an area of present-day Syria), the inscription describes Mesha, king of Moab, with the help of his god Chemosh, overthrowing the rule of Israel. King Omri of Israel, Ahab's father, is referred to by name in the inscription, and a number of biblical locations are also named. Significantly, it mentions the God of Israel, called "Yahweh."[15]

Daniel and Belshazzar

From a host of other discoveries, Daniel's account of the irreverent King Belshazzar stands out. Daniel names Belshazzar as the last king of Babylon. Yet all known Babylonian records listed Nabonidus as the last king. An obvious discrepancy—an error?

Then it was discovered in a Babylonian chronicle that Nabonidus inexplicably removed himself for a ten-year stint in Arabia, leaving the kingdom in the hands of his son Belshazzar. The confusion came because Nabonidus did not abdicate the kingship. He was still called king. Although Belshazzar was not the official king, Daniel and the Hebrew young men who were with him considered Belshazzar as the de facto king. Prior to the study of the Babylonian chronicles, Belshazzar had been mentioned only in the biblical record.

After his study of these findings, the archaeologist R.F. Dougherty concluded: "Of all non-Babylonian records dealing with the situation at the close of the Neo-Babylonian Empire, [the description of events in] . . . chapter five of the book of Daniel ranks next to cuneiform literature in accuracy."[16]

New Testament Verified

Archaeological research and discovery for the New Testament has been of a different nature than for the Old Testament. It is not so much a matter of digging for buried buildings or inscribed tablets; rather, New Testament archaeology is primarily a matter of existing written documents. F.F. Bruce comments:

> These documents may be *public or private inscriptions* on stone or some equally durable material: they may be papyri recovered from the sand of Egypt recording literary texts or housewives' shopping lists; they may be private notes scratched on fragments of unglazed pottery; they may be legends on coins preserving information about some otherwise forgotten government ruler or getting some point of official propaganda across to the people who used them.
>
> They may also represent a Christian *church's collection of sacred Scriptures*, like the Chester Beatty Biblical Papyri; they may be all that is left of the library of an ancient religious community, like the scrolls from Qumran or the Gnostic texts from Nag Hammadi. But whatever their character, they can be as important and relevant for the study of the New Testament as any cuneiform tablets are for the study of the Old.[17]

The common people wrote letters on papyrus and kept ordinary commercial accounts of life on it. An even cheaper writing material was broken pieces of pottery, called "ostraca." These were used for odd notes. If you want your notes kept for a thousand years, put it on ostraca!

Some pieces discovered in ancient rubbish heaps have shown the connection between the everyday language of the common people and the Greek in which most of the New Testament is written. Comparing these finds helps validate the differences between the Greek of classic literature and that of the New Testament. Through the discoveries of the papyri it is evident the New Testament Greek was quite similar to the language of the common people.

In 1931 the discovery of a collection of papyri texts of the Greek Scriptures, now known as the Chester Beatty Biblical Papyri, was made public. Once used by an outlying church in Egypt, it is folded and arranged like a bound book.

This collection comprises eleven fragmentary codices on leaves of papyrus paper, with three of the eleven containing most of the New Testament. One contained the four Gospels and the Book of Acts. A Pauline codex is the oldest of the eleven, and it was written at the beginning of the third century. It contains nine letters of Paul, the Epistle to the Hebrews, and Revelation.

Even in their present mutilated state, these papyri bear most important testimony to the early textual history of the New Testament.[18] As mentioned in chapter 6, the fragment of John's Gospel, dated around A.D. 100, is the oldest known fragment of any part of the New Testament.

Stone Inscriptions

Inscriptions on stone have been another source of valuable information. An example of this is an edict of Claudius inscribed on limestone at Delphi in central Greece. Again, F.F. Bruce writes:

This edict is to be dated [as originating] during the first seven months of A.D. 52, and mentions Gallio as being proconsul of Achaia. We know from other sources that Gallio's proconsulship lasted only for a year, and since proconsuls entered on their term of office on July 1, the inference is that Gallio entered his proconsulship on that date in A.D. 51. But Gallio's proconsulship of Achaia overlapped Paul's year and a half of ministry in Corinth (Acts 18:11-12) so that Claudius' inscription provides us with a fixed point for reconstructing the chronology of Paul's career."[19]

Luke, a well-respected historian, has been noted for his accuracy of detail. An example of his precision is his reference in Luke 3:1 to "Lysanias, the tetrarch of Abilene" or ruler of a quarter of a particular territory. This man was one of those in charge at the time when John the Baptist began his ministry in A.D. 27. Mention of Lysanias has been regarded as a mistake because the only ruler of that name known from ancient historians was King Lysanias, whom Antony executed at Cleopatra's instigation in 36 B.C., more than fifty years before John the Baptist.

Then, a Greek inscription from Abila (eighteen miles northwest of Damascus), from which the territory of Abilene is named, records a dedication to one Nymphaeus "free man of Lysanias, the tetrarch" between A.D. 14 and A.D. 29, around the very time indicated by Luke. Again, accuracy has been supported.[20]

No Pious Forgery

Archaeology confirms the accounts recorded by the Bible.

• *Coins* have provided some background information for parts of New Testament history. One of the crucial facts to establish the chronology of Paul's career is the date of Felix's replacement by Festus as procurator of Judea (Acts 24:27). A new Judean coinage began in Nero's fifth year, before October of A.D. 59. This may point to the beginning of the new procuratorship.

• *Sacred sites* have been definitely identified and general locations have also been uncovered. General locations have been more easily established than exact spots where some of the great New Testament events transpired.

> **Spiritual truth comes as we look beyond the archaeological finds to God Himself.**

• *Jerusalem* was destroyed in A.D. 70, and a new pagan city was established on the site in A.D. 135. This has complicated the identification of places in Jerusalem mentioned in the Gospels and Acts. Some, however, like the temple area and the Pool of

Siloam, to which our Lord sent the blind man to wash (John 9:11), have been clearly identified.

Archaeology is invaluable in helping us understand the Bible. It yields fascinating information that illuminates what might otherwise be obscured and in some instances confirms what some might otherwise regard as doubtful.

We can agree with Keith N. Schoville who says, "It is important to realize that archaeological excavations have produced ample evidence to prove unequivocally that the Bible is not a pious forgery. Thus far, no historical statement in the Bible has proven false on the basis of evidence retrieved through archaeologic research."[21]

Are Miracles Possible?

D o you really believe a whale swallowed Jonah? Do you seriously think that Jesus actually fed 5,000 people from five loaves of bread and two fish? So goes the thrust and tone of many modern questioners, who assume and frequently observe that these "miracle" stories in the Bible must be merely quaint ways of conveying spiritual truth.

As with all questions we have about God and His existence, the beginning is to discern the root—the underlying issue involved. Otherwise we discuss the twig, and not the major branch. This is especially true in understanding miracles. It is not the possibility of a particular miracle that is troubling, but with the whole principle. To establish the credibility of one miracle would not get to the root. The puzzle is with the whole possibility of miracles.

Our Concept of God

Questions about the credibility of miracles also extend to the validity of predictive prophecy or any supernatural act. All of these questions stem from a concept of a god who is conceived of as human, and not divine. Once we assume the existence and character of God, miracles are no longer a problem. God is by definition all-powerful. In the absence of such a God, the concept of miracles becomes difficult, if not impossible, to entertain.

This came to me very forcibly one day as I was talking about the deity of Christ with a Japanese professor friend. "I find it very difficult to believe," he said, "that a man could become God." Sensing his problem, I replied, "Yes, Kinichi, so do I, but I can believe that God could become a man." He instantly saw the difference, and not long afterward he saw the rationale of God in Christ coming to earth. He became a Christian.

Is God Bound by Natural Law?

Therefore, the question really is, Does an all-powerful God, who created the universe, exist? If so, we shall have little difficulty with miracles. If so, He transcends the natural law of which He is the Author. Reviewing our fundamental beliefs about God—that He is alive, active, powerful, and caring—will help our thinking about miracles.

Philosopher David Hume and others have defined a miracle as a violation of natural law. Such a position, however, for all practical purposes deifies natural law. Indeed, God thereby becomes the prisoner of natural law and, in effect, ceases to be God.

In this modern scientific age, it is common to personify science and natural law. This sidesteps the fact that these laws are merely the impersonal results of observation, sometimes even making natural law *the* deity. The Christian views natural law as behaving in an observable cause-and-effect way, all the time—year after year, century after century. At the same time, the Bible does not restrict God's right and power to intervene when and how He chooses. God is outside, over, and above natural law, and is not bound by it.

Natural laws do not cause anything in the sense that God causes and creates. These are merely descriptions of what we observe to be happening.

What Is a Miracle?

Miracle is a word used rather loosely today. If a scared student passes an exam, he says, "It was a miracle!" Or if our old car makes a successful trip from one city to another, we say, "It's a miracle the thing ran!" We use the term to mean anything that is unusual or unexpected. We do not necessarily mean that the hand of God has been at work.

Miracles, as recorded in the Bible, are acts of God. This is an entirely different sense than what we use in common speech. The biblical use is an act of God breaking into, changing, or interrupting the ordinary course of events.

• The Bible records various kinds of miracles, and some of them could have *a natural explanation*. For instance, the account in Exodus 14 tells of God parting a lane through the Red Sea to help the Israelites escape slavery from Egypt. Some have conjectured that the sea parted naturally because high winds drove the waters back. Perhaps this might have happened apart from God's intervention, but the miraculous part was the *timing*. The high winds would have had to come just when the Israelites reached the shore while the Egyptians were closing in on them in hot pursuit. Then after every Israelite was safely across and on the other side, the wind would have had to die down and prevented the Egyptians from following. The timing is the evidence of the miraculous intervention of God.

• On the other hand, there are many miracles for which *no natural explanation* arises. The resurrection of Lazarus from the dead and the resurrection of Jesus Christ both involved forces unknown to us and outside the realm of so-called natural law. The same is true of the record of Jesus' many healings.

• We might be tempted to explain Jesus' healings in terms of *psychosomatic response*, but the healings of Jesus were clearly outside this category. The healings of leprosy are a case in point. Obviously these healings were not psychosomatically based because the disease was caused from a bacterial invasion of the body. Lepers who were healed experienced the direct power of God. In addition, there are cases of congenital diseases

> **Jesus Himself is the one convincing and permanent miracle!**

being healed. The man born blind could not possibly be accounted for with a psychosomatic explanation. Nor could it have accounted for his receiving his sight (John 9).

• Another notion commonly expressed is that people in ancient times were exceedingly ignorant, gullible, and superstitious. No doubt they thought many things were miracles we now know were *not miracles at all but simply phenomena they did not understand*. Our understanding has expanded exponentially thanks to the benefits of modern science. For example, if we were to fly a modern jet over a primitive tribe today, they would probably fall to the ground in worship of this "silver-bird god" of the sky. They would think that the sight they observed was a miraculous phenomenon—a miracle. We would know that the plane is simply a result of the applied principles of aerodynamics, and there is nothing miraculous about it at all.

In the case of the blind man, there was a realistic view of his situation. The people observed that since the beginning of time it had not been known for a man born blind to receive his sight. They weren't dummies! And we have no more natural explanation of Jesus' healing him other than what the Gospels relate. And who, today, has any more explanation, in a natural sense, of Jesus' resurrection from the dead other than what evidence was available when it happened? No one! We simply cannot get away from the supernatural aspects of the biblical record.

No Conflict with Natural Law

It is important to note, however, that miracles are not in conflict with any natural law. Professor J.N. Hawthorne puts it this way: "Miracles are unusual events caused by God. The laws of nature are generalizations about ordinary events caused by him."[1]

There are two views among thinking Christians as to the relationship of miracles to natural law.

• First, miracles employ a "higher" natural law, which at present is

> **Miracles are not contrary to nature, but only contrary to what we know about nature.**

unknown to us. It is quite obvious that despite all of the impressive discoveries of modern science, we are still standing on the seashore of an ocean of ignorance. When our knowledge increases sufficiently, this thesis says we will realize that the things we thought today were miracles were merely the working of the higher laws of the universe, of which we were not aware at the time.

In the modern scientific sense, a law is that which is regular and acts uniformly. Therefore, if we say that a miracle is the result of a higher law, we are forced into a position in which we cannot admit to any deviation from natural law.

• Second, biblical miracles are the result of a sovereign, transcendent act of God's supernatural power. It seems that this is the more appropriate view.

Biblical Miracles

Biblical miracles were never capricious or fantastic, which is in contrast to miracle stories in pagan literature and those in other world religions. They were not scattered helter-skelter through the biblical record without rhyme or reason. There was always clear order and purpose to them. They cluster around three periods of biblical history:

- The Exodus,
- The prophets who led Israel, and
- The time of Christ and the early church.

In each of the biblical recordings of miracles, each one always had one purpose: to confirm faith in God. They authenticated the message and the messenger, or they demonstrated God's love by relieving suffering. They were never performed as entertainment—in the way a magician puts on a show for his or her patrons.

Miracles were never performed for personal prestige or to gain money or power. The Devil tempted Jesus in the wilderness to use His divine power in just this way, but Jesus steadfastly refused. Instead, Jesus referred to the centrality of God in the use of any demonstration of miracles (see Luke 4:1-13).

In answer to the direct request of the Jewish rulers to tell them plainly whether He was the Messiah, Jesus replied, "I did tell you, but you do not believe. The miracles I do in my Father's name speak for me" (John 10:25). Again Jesus said if they had any hesitation in believing His claims, they should believe Him "on the evidence of the miracles themselves" (14:11).

In addition, God used miracles in the fledgling Christian church to confirm the Christian message, which repeatedly centered on the miracle of Jesus' resurrection. (Note these incidents as recorded in the Book of Acts.)

Why Not Now?

People often argue, "If God performed miracles in the past, why doesn't He do them now? If I saw a miracle, I could believe!" Jesus Himself answered this question.

He told a story about a rich man who was in the torment of hell. This man lifted up his eyes and pleaded with Abraham that someone should warn his five brothers lest they too should come into this awful place. Abraham then told this man that his brothers had the Scriptures. But the rich man protested that if someone should rise from the dead, they would be shaken by the miracle and would turn from their worldly lifestyle. The reply given sadly applies as much today as then: "If they do not listen to Moses and the Prophets, they will not be convinced even if someone rises from the dead" (Luke 16:31).

Jesus' statement speaks to us today in the midst of the pressure of our contemporary cultural norms. Yet, without our awareness and acceptance of the spiritual realm, our rationalistic presuppositions tend to rule out the very possibility of miracles. Our postmodernistic thinking tells us miracles are impossible, and no amount of evidence can ever persuade us one has taken place. Instead, we automatically advance a naturalistic explanation to those events that baffle us.

The biblical miracles are always purposeful, however. A number of times the people who saw Jesus' power asked for more magic or wizardry, but He repeatedly asserted that His sole purpose was to teach spiritual truth and to demonstrate His own character and His "Father's" power. His self-definition was to give us Life, abundant Life, and to reveal God. "Grace and truth came through Jesus Christ" were the Apostle John's words (John 1:17). Each miracle was toward this end.

Reliable Records Verify the Miracles

Miracles are not necessary for us today as a basis of faith in Christ because we have extraordinary records of superior accuracy to show us God's truth. As Bernard Ramm observes, "If miracles are capable of sensory perception, they can be made matters of [written] testimony. If they are adequately investigated, the recorded testimony has the same validity for evidence as the experience of beholding the event."[2]

Every court in the world operates on the basis of reliable testimony by word of mouth or in writing. "If the raising of Lazarus was actually witnessed by John and recorded truthfully by him when still in soundness of faculties and memory, for purposes of evidence it is the same as if we were there and saw it."[3] Ramm then lists reasons we may know that the miracles have adequate and reliable testimony. To summarize:

• Jesus' miracles were *done in public*. They were not performed in secret before only one or two people, who then announced them to the world. There was every opportunity to investigate the miracles on the spot. It is very impressive that the opponents of Jesus *never denied* the fact of the miracles He performed. They either attributed them to the power of Satan or else tried to suppress the evidence, as with the raising of Lazarus from the dead. They said, in effect, "Let's kill Him before the people realize what is happening and the whole world goes after Him!"

• Jesus' miracles were *done before nonbelievers*. By contrast, miracles claimed by cults and offbeat groups never seem to happen when the skeptic is present to observe. This was not true with Jesus.

• Jesus' miracles were *carried out over a period of time*, during which He *demonstrated a variety of powers*. He had power over nature, as when He turned water into wine. He had power over disease, as when He healed the lepers and the blind. He had power over demons, as was shown by His casting them out of people. He had supernatural knowledge, as in His knowing that Nathaniel was under a fig tree. He displayed His power to create when He fed 5,000 people from a few loaves and fish. He had power over natural forces as when He calmed the wind and the waves of a strong storm. And finally, He exhibited power over death itself in the raising of Lazarus and others from the dead.

• The *testimony of the cured* is undeniable. As noted earlier, we have it from those, like Lazarus, whose healings could not have been psychosomatic or a result of inaccurate diagnosis.

• These New Testament accounts of Jesus of Nazareth are *extraordinarily unique*—in a entirely different category contrasted to non-Christian religions. They are but a part of an entire, authentic message: His birth, His message of forgiveness, His death, and His resurrection.

Miracles are believed in non-Christian religions because the religion is already believed, but in the biblical religion, miracles are part of the means of establishing the true religion. This distinction is of immense importance. A series of miracles brought the nation of Israel into existence, and supernatural wonders pervade the first five books of the Old Testament. Many of the prophets were identified as God's spokesmen by their power to perform miracles. Jesus came not only preaching but also performing miracles, and His apostles from time to time worked wonders. It was the miracle authenticating the religion at every point.[4]

C.S. Lewis affirms, "All the essentials of Hinduism would, I think, remain unimpaired if you subtracted the miraculous, and the same is almost true of Islam, but you cannot do that with Christianity. It is precisely the story of a great miracle. *A naturalistic Christianity leaves out all that is specifically Christian.*"[5]

Pagan Miracles

Miracles recorded outside the Bible differ in order, dignity, and motive from those in Judeo-Christian Scripture. What is more important, however, is the amazing, solid authentication contained in biblical miracles (discussed in chapter 6). Similar investigations into both secular and pagan records of miracles show that comparable authentication is lacking. The more we integrate facts into our thinking, the more accurate will be our judgment of all truth claims.

Using the same standards for judging the alleged miracles and healings we hear in our time aids our thinking. In fact, the consistency and authentication of biblical miracles can become the standard by which we judge all other so-called miracles and alleged healings of our time. You will see that they do not stand the full weight of investigation. A summary exposure will show they are not equal to biblical miracles.

Nevertheless, the discovery that some miracles are counterfeit is no proof that all are spurious, any more than the discovery of counterfeit currency would prove all currency spurious.

Exaggerated Reporting

Some attempts have been made to explain away miracles on the basis of exaggerated reporting, especially by Jesus' followers. In general, we could say people are notoriously inaccurate in reporting events and impressions. Play the simple party game of "Rumor" in which a secret is whispered from person to person around

> **Miracles do not appear on the pages of Scripture vagrantly. They appear when God is speaking to His people through accredited messengers.**

a room and see how the details change through transmission. In light of such a tendency, some say it is obvious the reliability of any human being as an observer may be easily discounted; and on this basis, we can discount the Gospel accounts of miracles as the mistaken observations of inaccurate and imaginative observers.

Despite our unintentional tendency to distort and exaggerate, our law courts have not ceased functioning, and eyewitnesses are still considered able to provide highly useful information. Although there may be some question about an automobile accident, eyewitnesses can still furnish such details as the time, speed of the cars, location, and so on. Moreover, the accident cannot be said *not* to have happened just because of the discrepancies in witnesses' stories. As Ramm observes, the smashed cars and the injured people are irrefutable evidence on which all agreed.[6]

Of course, we note that there may be limitations to investigating any given assertion, such as the reliability of the witnesses. If we press every consideration that might help us see an assertion more clearly to the outer limits, we will inevitably refute that very assertion. For instance, those conducting the reliability or unreliability of a human witness are assuming their own reliability. Put another way, if one person says another's testimony is unreliable, there is the equal possibility his or her own testimony is likewise unreliable.

Were Biblical Believers Objective?

One questionable idea, sometimes advanced, is that the miracle stories must be discarded because believing disciples told them, and therefore what they said was not objective. The disciples, however, were the ones on the scene who saw the miracles. The fact that they were disciples is neither here nor there. The question is, Did they tell the *truth?* As we have seen, eyewitness testimony is the best we can get, and most of the disciples faced the specter of death as the test of their veracity.

In our courts of law, we would not say that in order to guarantee objectivity on the part of witnesses, we will listen only to those who were not at the scene of an accident and had nothing to do with it. Nor would we say we would not take testimony from eyewitnesses or victims, claiming they would be prejudiced. The crucial question in each case is truthfulness, not proximity or relationship to the events.

The Question Is Philosophical

The fundamental question of whether miracles are possible is not scientific, but philosophical. Science can only say that miracles do not occur in the ordinary course of nature. *Science cannot forbid miracles because natural laws do not cause, and therefore cannot forbid, anything.* Natural laws, as we see them, are merely descriptions of what happens.

The Christian also embraces the concept of natural law. "It is essential to the theistic doctrine of miracles that nature be uniform [predictable] in her daily routine. If nature were utterly spontaneous [unpredictable], miracles would be as impossible to detect as it would be to establish a natural law."[7]

This difference between the Christian and the scientist is philosophical because each has distinctive presuppositions, the base of all our opinions. The possibility of seeing something as a miracle, therefore, depends on our presuppositions, our point of view, or our worldview.

What then is the presupposition of the Christian? *God exists, has originated natural law, can make or break it, and can intervene or not.* The supernatural, personal God is at the base of all phenomenon, natural and spiritual. G.K. Chesterton said, "A miracle is startling; but it is simple. It is simple because it is a miracle. It is power coming directly from God instead of indirectly through nature or human wills."[8]

What, then, is the presupposition of the scientist? *God does not, can-*

not exist. Scientists (unless they are Christian) generally make all judgments and opinions based on naturalistic, materialistic observations, believing there is no other option. From this presupposition the supernatural does not intrude, and indeed, would not be considered. The scientist, like anyone else, can only ask, "Are the records of miracles historically reliable?" He or she will go no further.

As a summary of thoughts on miracles, we have seen the miracles in the Bible as an inherent part of God's communication to us—not a mere appendage with little significance. It also takes us back again to the ultimate question: Does God exist? Settle that question and miracles cease to be a problem. The very uniformity against which a miracle stands in stark contrast depends on an omnipotent Author of natural law, who is also capable of transcending it to accomplish His sovereign ends.

Do Science and Scripture Agree?

I f ever there was a question that has generated more heat than light, it is the question: Do science and Scripture agree? No doubt there is conflict. On the one hand, there are Christians who make the Bible say things it really does not say, and on the other hand, there are scientists who claim their philosophical interpretation is the same as the scientific facts (scientism). Their interpretations, however, are distinct from the facts themselves.

To the question, Have some scientists and Christians disagreed? the answer would have to be a resounding yes! To know this is the case, we need only recall

- the church's persecution of Galileo for claiming the sun revolved around the earth,
- the Scopes trial of 1925 about teaching creation or evolution in the schools,

- or the confrontation on slavery a century ago between Wilberforce and Huxley.

Well-Meaning Christians

As we have indicated, part of the problem stems from some well-meaning but misguided Christians who make the Bible say what it does not say. One classic and harmful example is the Bible chronology calculated by Bishop James Ussher (1581–1656), a contemporary of Shakespeare. He worked out a series of dates from the genealogies in the Bible and concluded the world was created in 4004 B.C.

Many skeptics, including the famous Lord Bertrand Russell, thought that Christians actually believe Creation occurred in 4004 B.C. Some time ago I was visiting a student at a Midwestern state university campus. He picked up a true-false exam from his course on Western civilization. One question read, "According to the Bible, the world was created in 4004 B.C."

"I suppose your instructor wants you to mark this question true," I said.

"That's right," the student replied.

"Interesting," I mused. Pulling an Oxford edition of the Bible from my pocket, I said, "I wonder if you could show me where the Bible says that."

The student was puzzled that he couldn't find the date on the first page of Genesis. Trying to be helpful, a Christian student who was with me volunteered, "It's on page 3."

It was news to both of them that Bishop Ussher's dates, which appear in some English Bibles, are not part of the original text.

On the other hand, some scientists have been known to make statements beyond the facts. These statements are philosophical interpretations of data that do not carry the same weight of authority as hard data. Unfortunately, the facts and the interpretations are seldom distinguished in the minds of listeners.

When a Scientist Speaks

When scientists speak on any subject, they are likely to be believed. They may be speaking outside their field, but the same respect given to their statements within their field are almost unconsciously transferred to everything they say. Who can argue with such erudition? For instance,

Carl Sagan, a well-known author and late professor of astronomy at Cornell University, illustrates this crossover from science to "scientism" (a personal philosophical opinion). *U.S. News & World Report* interviewed him on the subject of science and religion. Science is his field; religion certainly is not! However, he makes bold religious pronouncements: "The cosmos is all that is or ever was or ever will be"; "Whatever significance we humans have is that which we make ourselves"; and "If we must worship a power greater than ourselves, does it not make sense to worship the sun and the stars?" But why would we worship nature, if it is, as he states, "the result of blind chance and part of a pointless process"?[1]

Faith Is Suspect

Another area in which conflict has arisen is on the question of whether those things that the scientific method cannot verify are valid and real. Some people consciously, and others unconsciously, assume that if the methods of natural science cannot prove a statement in a laboratory, it is untrustworthy and cannot be accepted as reliable. The findings of science are considered to be objective and therefore real; whereas statements that must be accepted by faith are looked on as suspect.

E.C. Wilson, widely respected astronomer, illustrates this position in his book *On Human Nature*. He states, "The final decisive edge enjoyed by scientific naturalism will come from its capacity to explain traditional religion, its chief competitor [sic], as a wholly material phenomenon."[2]

But there are ways and means other than the laboratory to acquire real and genuine knowledge. Consider the process of falling in love. This surely is not done in a laboratory with a battery of instruments, but anyone who has ever experienced it would be the last to admit that his or her knowledge of love is uncertain or unreal. Other presuppositions of science include the existence of truth, laws of logic, the adequacy of language, and numbers. The simple fact is that true, rationally justified beliefs exist in a host of fields outside of science.[3] The scientific method is valid only for those realities that are measurable in physical terms.

God is a different kind of reality from the world of nature that science examines. God does not await someone's empirical investigation; He is a personal being who has revealed Himself in love and can be known in personal presence.

The Scientist Uses Faith

Faith is no detriment to the apprehension of reality. In fact, science itself rests on presuppositions that must be accepted by faith before research is possible.

- *The universe is orderly.* It operates according to a pattern, and therefore it can be examined and its behavior can be predicted. This would include the uniformity of our world, and that it will continue as it is currently; for example, apples will always fall down, not up.

- *Objective truth exists and is knowable.* The object of the scientist's faith is solely materialistic and naturalistic; all of its efforts are confined to these naturalistic phenomena. One might say the scientist's truth will not extend beyond these visible areas. The presupposition is that things that cannot be examined under a microscope or with a telescope undoubtedly do not exist.

- *The reliability of the sense perceptions is another nonphysical presupposition that must be accepted by faith.* One must believe that our senses are trustworthy enough in order to get a true picture of the universe and enable us to understand its orderliness.

- *The repeatability of a laboratory experiment is also a matter of faith.* When a work by a scientist gets published and is repeated by another scientist, the results will be the same. Put hydrogen and oxygen together in the proper proportions, you will get water—given the same conditions.

It should be observed here that the scientific method, as we know it today, began in the sixteenth century among people who were Christians. They broke with the Greek polytheistic concepts, which viewed the universe as capricious and irregular, and therefore not capable of systematic study. The Christian scientists, however, reasoned that the universe must be orderly and worthy of investigation because it was the work of an intelligent Creator. In pursuing scientific research, they were convinced they were thinking God's thoughts after Him.

Both Sides Have Presuppositions

Christians have a worldview, a *presupposition*, through which they filter all other information as well. We believe science is one avenue for the discovery of truth . . . with a capital T. Also, God exists, is active in His creation, and is our seminal frame of reference. A Christian sees nothing incompatible with reason or intelligence to have faith in the supernatural God. Those Christians who are scientists do not consider themselves intellectual schizophrenics, but rather view themselves as following in the footsteps of the Christian founders of modern science.

Widely quoted, William Paley couched this view for us in the eighteenth century·

> Suppose I had found a watch upon the ground, and it should be inquired how the watch happened to be in that place. I should hardly think the answer would be . . . the watch must have always been there. Of course, the watch must have had a maker, that existed before, an artificer who formed it for the purpose which we find it; someone who comprehended its construction and designed its use.[4]

This expresses the Christian's presupposition. God, the Creator, existed *before* the world was made, and He was and is "an artificer," who formed it and designed it. Science, along with any other data, is seen through this God-focused filter.

The entire revelation of the Bible is built on this premise—God has revealed Himself, and He is the Creator. Jesus said, "You will know the truth, and the truth will set you free" (John 8:32). It *is* possible to differentiate between truth and error.

The agnostic (or atheistic) scientist, on the other hand, also has a presupposition, but one that is quite different than the Christian's. Even with the most detailed, complex discoveries, Darwin's basic evolutionary mechanism strongly persists and is even fought for. Random variation (mutation) and natural selection are theories still clung to. Atheist Richard Dawkins claims that everything, including our minds, can be "reduced" to its material base. He says, "We are survival machines—robot vehicles blindly programmed to preserve the selfish molecules (of DNA which survived) known as genes." Later, he seemed to have second thoughts as he says, "The objects and phenomena that a physics book describes are simpler than a single cell in the body of its author."[5]

The impact of Paley's "artificer" Watchmaker still persists and provoked not a little attention with its unarguable logic. Taking up the argument, self-described atheist Dawkins authored the book *The Blind Watchmaker*. To disparage the "Artificer" idea for the existence of the watch, he champions natural selection: "It has no mind and no mind's eye. It does not plan for the future. It has no vision, no foresight, no sight at all. If it can be said to play the role of watchmaker in nature, it is the *blind* watchmaker!"[6]

The Black Box Opened

The continuing discussions using the "watchmaker" analogy have brought to fore the inscrutability and even wonderment regarding the details of natural life. Michael Behe, molecular biologist, in his book *Darwin's Black Box* opens up the interior of the molecule, originally thought of as a single proton and neutron. With our powerful microscopes and testing expertise, the Black Box of Darwin's single cell has shown a new world in microscopic detail. One sample of Behe's illustrations explains the molecular complexity necessary for the retina of the eye to accommodate and rearrange itself when light enters it.

When light first strikes the retina, a photon interacts with a molecule

---

Three examples of "irreducible complexity"

DNA—Molecules that hold the blueprints for the construction of life.

RNA—Molecules that carry the blueprints from the DNA to specific proteins.

PROTEINS— Molecules that follow portions of the blueprints in building and repairing life molecules.

---

called 11-cis retinal, which rearranges it to trans-retinal within picoseconds. (A picosecond is about the time it takes light to travel the breadth of a single human hair.)[7]

Other similar illustrations can be cited. The meticulous function of the estimated 100,000 genes of the human genetic blueprint screams loudly of an intelligent programmer. Our DNA, proteins, and RNA are information banks holding in detail our personal characteristics: our height, hair and eye color, fingerprint, brain cells, and so on. Each human being, except for identical twins, holds his or her own profile. Made up of spiral chemical ladders, they are so intricate and unique that Behe concludes that a Designer is firmly indicated. His memorable term for the human genome is "irreducible complexity," *nothing can be left out*.[8]

Behe illustrated the idea of the "irreducibility" of a molecule in the construction of a simple mousetrap. The piece of wood, the spring, the lever for the cheese all must be there. Take out one part, and you will not catch a mouse. Similarly, a molecule has irreducible complexity, albeit, a thousand times more complex than a mousetrap.

Molecular mechanisms are as obviously designed as a spaceship or a computer. You cannot explain the origin of any biological capability (like vision) unless you can explain the molecular mechanisms that make it work.[9]

Could such complexity come together by the chance appearance of the essential molecules at the same time and place? It is beyond the realm of natural possibility. Nonetheless, Darwinian evolutionary scientists find an "intelligent cause" unthinkable even while examining such extraordinary complexity.

Check Out the Meaning of Evolution

Whenever the term *evolution* is used, it helps to understand your own intended meaning. In addition, find out what others mean when they use the word. At the risk of oversimplification, we will consider three general views of evolution.

• The first view can be called *evolutionism*. Those who hold this worldview believe the universe has been evolving forever on the basis of natural processes, mutation, and natural selection. Relying on chance, it is the "survival of the fittest."

• The second view is called *microevolution*, which describes a continued process of change or development within a species. In connection with this, it's important to understand that a species is one of seven classifications of all living plants and animals, listed by Swedish naturalist Carolus Linnaeus. The groups are (1) kingdom, (2) phylum, (3) class, (4) order, (5) family, (6) genus, and (7) species. The kingdom is the largest group and the species is the smallest. Members of a species have a high degree of similarity among themselves and generally interbreed only among themselves. G.A. Kerkut, an evolutionist, described it as "many living animals observed over the course of time which undergo change so that new [varieties] are formed."[10] Note that the emphasis for this view is on "within a species."

According to proponents of microevolution, these changes may be chromosome changes, gene mutations, or hybridization to produce new varieties within a species. The changes have always remained within their species. As has been said, "A horse is still a horse." Or *"No protozoa to a man."*

To illustrate, if a mutation takes place within the genes of the earthworm, providing it with increased dexterity against predatory blackbirds, the carriers of this mutation will fare better in the earthworm's struggle for survival. This mutation will improve the worm—but strictly as a worm. This is microevolution within a single species.

Microevolution will allow for creation of new species, but not the development of one species to a higher classification. Most contemporary Christian scholars would agree that this kind of evolution takes place.

Yet we may logically ask if the Genesis word *kind* is the same as species (Gen. 1:21, 24). Dr. Kenneth Kantzer, author and theologian, states this word is not. It is "simply 'kind' in a most general way, and could apply to anything from a Linnean phylum to a Linnean species. It is even pressing too much into the phrase 'after its kind' to interpret it to mean that God individually created each 'kind' by a separate act . . . [but] each kind reproduces offspring like itself."[11]

• The third view is *macroevolution*, also called megaevolution, which requires the transfer of genetic information to a higher, more complex classification—the boundaries being crossed by mutation and natural selection.

A.E. Wilder-Smith, professor of pharmacology, points out that these factors along with chance "cannot provide the information necessary to build *legs onto a fish*, thus permitting it to leave the water and to walk on land. Paleontology, for example, knows of no missing links (transitional forms) between whales and land mammals that have ever been established. Intermediate links of this sort would probably have been incapable of living. For over 120 years geology has been searching for these links in vain."[12] Actually, it is erroneous to speak of *the* missing link. Theoretically, there should be thousands of missing links!

Many scholars recognize that science is incapable of making *value judgments* about the things it measures. Many people on the frontiers of science are realizing that there is nothing inherent in science to guide them in the application of the discoveries they make. There is nothing in science itself that will determine whether nuclear energy will be used to destroy cities or destroy cancer. This is a judgment to be determined outside the scientific method.

Science can tell us how something works but not why it works that way. Whether there is any purpose in the universe can never be answered for us by science. As one writer put it: "Science can give us the 'know-how,' but it cannot give us the know-why.' "[13] We are dependent on revelation for many kinds of information, the absence of which leaves us with a quite incomplete picture.

How Does God Fit In?

Some have erroneously thought God was necessary only when life and existence have no other explanation. Unbelieving scientists seize on this concept to point out that the gaps are narrowing. "Give us enough time," they say, "and humans will be able to explain how everything in the universe works."

This point of view cannot fit into the description we saw in chapter 2. The God who made this world is not only Creator but also Sustainer. "He is before all things, and in him all things hold together" (Col. 1:17). The universe would fall apart without His *sustaining power*. Should science determine how the universe is sustained or discover the mechanism that keeps it going, this is not the same as being able to sustain it. For instance, we understand some things about the function of light, but who of us is capable of generating its incredible speed of travel? Suppose God took His sustaining power from the universe entirely. Let's give that a thought!

A commonly asked question is whether God could have made the world and used the process of evolution to do it. Phillip Johnson counters, however, by noting that this would mean God made the laws, set up the physical structures, and then retired. This view is called *deism*. One necessary question would be what is meant by evolution. By its common definition, evolution is mindless, unguided, purposeless, and solely material. God would have no place in this process. Nor does the biblical account of a personal God fit this image.

Theism, on the other hand, sees God as both Creator and actively involved in the world and the people He made. He is invisible but nonetheless real and involved with this world.[14]

Advances made recently in the fields of genetic engineering, microbiology, astrophysics, and so on are evoking undreamed of possibilities and possibly new questions for science. Three basic thoughts merit our attention:

- Life consists of not only *matter* (chemicals) but also *information.*
- Where (or from whom) did the information originate?
- Complex, specified information comes from an intelligent mind.

The advances in science give credence to the fact that life did not come by blind chance, but by an intelligent mind, the result of superior knowledge. Recent discoveries would argue for theism rather than blind chance. And, of course, where did the original elements of life come from? Could they have merely evolved? Now called the "soup theory," this view asserts that life began in a primordial sauce of chemicals, but the theory is now being questioned. The most logical explanation is that God created those elements.

Science and Scripture Moving Closer?

Some new developments in science have supported the Christian position in surprising ways. This does not mean the scientists have all become theists, but there are a number of areas where there is agreement on both biblical and scientific issues.

- In April of 1992, news media and scientists from around the globe proclaimed a great breakthrough. The Cosmic Background Explorer (COBE) satellite found a "stunning confirmation of the *hot big bang* creation event."

"It's the most exciting thing that's happened in my lifetime," stated Carlos Frank of Durham University in Britain.

"It is the discovery of the century, if not of all time," declared Stephen Hawking.

"It's like looking at God. We have found the evidence for the birth of the universe," said George Smoot of the University of California.

These reactions, of course, refer to the discovery of the big bang, the beginning of the universe. Basically, the hot big bang model says the entire physical universe—all matter and energy and even the four dimensions of space and time—burst forth from a state of infinite or near infinite density, temperature, and pressure.[15] The universe expanded from a volume very much smaller than the period at the end of this sentence [sic], and now continues to expand.[16]

• *The beginning of time.* God exists outside of our time as we know it. Even Stephen Hawking said, "Time itself must have a beginning."[17] The early chapters of Genesis tell the story of a God who existed before and apart from the time and universe He created. He is not subject to length, width, height, and time. He is the one who brought them into existence.

• *God caused effects even before time.* "In the beginning God created the heaven and the earth" (Gen. 1:1). Then, "For by him all things were created: things in heaven and on earth, visible and invisible. . . . He is before all things, and in him all things hold together" (Col. 1:16-17). He existed long before He uttered the words, "Let there be light." We are finite; we have a beginning. He is infinite; He has no beginning and no end.

BIBLICAL STATEMENTS OF COSMOLOGICAL SIGNIFICANCE

• God existed "before the universe," yet can be in it. (Col. 1:16-17)
• Time has a beginning. God precedes time. (2 Tim. 1:9)
• Jesus Christ created the universe. He has no beginning and was not created. (John 1:3)
• God created the universe from what our five senses cannot detect. (Heb. 11-13)
• Jesus evidenced His extra-dimensionality after His resurrection. He passed through walls. (John 20:26-28)
• God is very near, yet we cannot see Him. He is extra-dimensional. (Deut. 30:11-14)
• God designed the universe in a way to support human beings. (Neh. 9:6)

Hugh Ross,
The Creation Hypothesis

• *Fine-tuning of the cosmic constants.* The fixed cosmic laws of both our solar system and the entire universe make it possible for life on our planet. These laws are so precise that we could not exist even if any one of them varied the most minute fraction. J.P. Moreland has listed twenty-five of these that affect the earth's temperature, our seasons, and our entire atmosphere. If these were adjusted just a hair, sometimes by as much as a millionth of a percent, no life would be possible.[18]

A few of these are evident to us: the strength of gravity, the axial tilt, oxygen-to-nitrogen ratio in the atmosphere, ozone level, seismic activity, carbon dioxide and water vapor levels, the speed of the stars flying apart from one another, expansion of the universe, the velocity of light, entropy level of the universe, the force of electricity, the mass of the proton, and on and on. The existence of these factors is testimony to the unlikelihood that chance kept them constant.

• *The origin of life information justifies the claim that there had to be an intelligent mind that preexisted it.* The DNA and RNA studies that we've already considered point again to a Designer.

Origin of the Human Species

When we consider evolution and the origins of human beings, the Bible gives two nonnegotiables: God supernaturally and deliberately created the heavens and the earth (Gen. 1:1), and God supernaturally and deliberately created the first man and the first woman (v. 27). We do not shrink from these two limits. The Genesis account tells us God made Adam and then made Eve from Adam's side, both "made in God's image." When God breathed into Adam the breath of life, that set him apart from anything else God had made. This was a first! It also rules out the possibility suggested by some that people evolved from any animal ancestor.

It is helpful to read the New Testament references that confirm Adam and Eve as historic firsts (Rom. 5:12, 14; 1 Cor. 15:22, 45; 2 Cor. 11:3; 1 Tim. 2:13-14; Jude 11). A careful understanding of these passages leaves no room for the possibility that the Genesis account is mere allegory.

Francis Schaeffer profoundly affirms: "God gave us religious truths in a book of history and a book that touches on the cosmos as well. What sense does it make for God to give us religious truths and at the same time place them in a book that is wrong when it touches history and the cosmos?"[19]

What about the Age of the Earth?

From the biblical record, some Christians assume the earth must have been created not too many thousands of years before the birth of Christ. Yet they believe from science that the earth must be millions or billions of years old and feel squeamish about it. The question is, Can we date the earth from the biblical records?

Let's look at the use of the Hebrew word *day*. Can it mean periods of time rather than a single twenty-four hour day? In Genesis 1:31 the word is used to describe the completion of the sixth day during which God created Adam and Eve.

Genesis 2:15-25 describes God's creative activity on that "day." It also describes Adam's activity: naming *all* the animals, falling into a deep sleep, the creation of Eve—all on the sixth day! It seems that even with the most literal interpretation of this day, the sixth day was longer than twenty-four hours.

The use of the same word in other passages shows the Lord's concept of day is not so confined. For instance, "A thousand years in your sight are like a day that has just gone by" (Ps. 90:4) and "With the Lord a day is like a thousand years" (2 Peter 3:8). Theologian Davis Young notes that "the language of Genesis 1 (for example, the development of vegetation on day three) strongly implies the processes of natural growth and development, initiated by the decree of God's word ('Let the land produce vegetation')."

It should be noted that some erudite evangelical scholars interpret the Genesis account as describing twenty-four hour days, with God creating a "grown-up" universe within that time frame. And we need to consider their arguments. However, Young speaks to this: "The Christian geologist need not assume that all geological features were created with an appearance of age. He may assume that rocks, mountains, and other geological features of the six days of creation were formed through processes analogous with those of the present. And he has the right to use evidence contained in those rocks to reconstruct the past by analogy with the present. This also helps us avoid the problem of why God should have created a rock deposit that looked as if it had been formed by glacial action but really had not."[20]

In summary, Kantzer states, "As biblical students, therefore, we must remain agnostic about the age of the earth. We have no biblical warrant for ruling out the validity of the commonly accepted geological timetable. Let scientists battle it out on the basis of the scientific evidence, but we should not bolster weak scientific positions with misinterpretations of the Bible conjured up for that purpose. God rarely sees fit merely to gratify our curiosity."[21] In matters where God chooses to be silent, we should likewise choose to remain silent.

A Constantly Moving Train

Scientific theory is a matter of the highest degree of probability based on the available data. There are no absolutes in it. Furthermore, science is a train that is constantly moving. Yesterday's generalization is today's discarded hypothesis. This is one reason for being somewhat tentative about accepting any form of evolutionary theory as the final explanation of biology. It is also why it has become dangerous to try to prove the Bible by science. If the Bible becomes wedded to today's scientific theories, what will happen to it when science has shifted ten years from now?

Theologian W.A. Criswell states, "In 1861 . . . the French Academy of Science published a little brochure in which they stated fifty-one scientific facts that controverted the Word of God. Today there is not a scientist in the world who believes a single one of those fifty-one so-called scientific facts that in 1861 were published as controverting the Word of God. Not a one!"[22]

Thoughtful evolutionists concede that the matter is not an open-and-shut case, but they feel the theory must be accepted despite some seeming contradictions and unexplained factors. G.A. Kerkut, an evolutionist, writes of his perspective that theology students at Cambridge in a former century had placidly accepted dogma and teachings they did not personally investigate. Kerkut then observes that some present-day students have done likewise. He writes:

For some years now I have tutored undergraduates on various aspects of biology. It is quite common, during the course of conversation, to ask the student if he knows the evidence for evolution. This usually evokes a faintly superior smile. . . . "Well, sir, there is the evidence from paleontology, comparative anatomy, embryology, systematic and geographical distributions," the student would say in a nursery-rhyme jargon. . . .

"Do you think that the evolutionary theory is the best explanation yet advanced to explain animal interrelationships?" I would ask.

"Why, of course, sir," would be the reply. "There is nothing else, except for the religious explanation held by some fundamentalist Christians, and I gather, sir, that these views are no longer held by the more up-to-date churchmen."

"So you believe in evolution because there is no other theory?"

"Oh, no, sir, I believe in it because of the evidence I just mentioned."

"Have you read any book on the evidence for evolution?" I would ask.

"Yes, sir." And here he would mention the names of authors of a popular school textbook. "And of course, sir, there is that book by Darwin, *The Origin of Species*."

"Have you read this book?" I would ask.

"Well, not all through, sir."

"The first fifty pages?"

"Yes, sir, about that much; maybe a bit less."

"I see. And that has given you your firm understanding of evolution?"

"Yes, sir."

"Well, now, if you really understand an argument you will be able to indicate to me not only the points in favor of the argument, but also the most telling points against it."

"I suppose so, sir."

"Good. Please tell me, then, some of the evidence against the theory of evolution."

"But there isn't any, sir."

Here the conversation would take on a more strained atmosphere. The student would look at me as if I were playing a very unfair game. He would take it rather badly when I suggest that he was not being very scientific in his outlook if he swallowed the latest scientific dogma and, when questioned, just repeated parrot-fashion the views of the current Archbishop Evolution. In fact he would be behaving like certain of those religious students he affected to despise. He would be taking on faith what he could not intellectually understand and, when questioned, would appeal to authority of a "good book," which in this case was *The Origin of Species*. (It is interesting to note that many of these widely quoted books are read by title only. Three of such that come to mind are the Bible, *The Origin of Species*, and *Das Kapital*.)

I would suggest that the student should go away and read the evidence for and against evolution and present it as an essay. A week would pass and the same student would appear armed with an essay on the evidence for evolution. The essay would usually be well done, since the student might have realized that I should be rough to convince. When the essay had been read and the question concerning the evidence against evolution came up, the student would give a rather pained smile. "Well, sir, I looked up various books but could not find anything in the scientific books against evolution. I did not think you would want a religious argument."

"No, you were quite correct. I want a scientific argument against evolution."

"Well, sir, there does not seem to be one, and that in itself is a piece of evidence in favor of the evolutionary theory."

I would then indicate to him that the theory of evolution was of considerable antiquity, and would mention that he might have looked at the book by Radi, *The History of Biological Theories*. Having made sure the student had noted the book down for future reference I would proceed as follows:

Before one can decide that the theory of evolution is the best explanation of the present-day range of forms of living material, one should examine all the implications that such a theory may hold. Too often the theory is applied to, say, the development of the horse, and then, because it is held to be applicable there, it is extended to the rest of the animal kingdom with little or no further evidence.

There are, however, seven basic assumptions that are often not mentioned during discussions of evolution. Many evolutionists ignore the first six assumptions and consider only the seventh.

The first assumption is that nonliving things gave rise to living material, i.e., that spontaneous generation occurred.

The second assumption is that spontaneous generation occurred only once.

The third . . . is that viruses, bacteria, plants, and animals are all interrelated.

The fourth . . . is that the protozoa gave rise to the metazoa.

The fifth . . . is that the various invertebrate phyla are interrelated.

The sixth . . . is that the invertebrates gave rise to the vertebrates.

The seventh . . . is that the vertebrates and fish gave rise to the amphibia, the amphibia to the reptiles, and the reptiles to the birds and mammals. Sometimes this is expressed in other words, i.e., that the modern amphibia and reptiles had a common ancestral stock and so on.

For the initial purposes of this discussion on evolution I shall consider that the supporters of the theory of evolution hold that all these seven assumptions are valid, and that these assumptions form the general theory of evolution.

The first point that I should like to make is that the seven assumptions by their nature are not capable of experimental verification. They assume that a certain series of events has occurred in the past. Thus, though it may be possible to mimic some of these events under present-day conditions, this does not mean that these events must therefore have take place in the past. All that it shows is that it is possible for such a change to take place. Thus, to change a present-day reptile into a mammal, though of great interest, would not show the way in which the mammals did arise. Unfortunately, we cannot bring about even this change; instead we have to depend upon limited circumstantial evidence for our assumptions.[23]

Keeping the Facts Straight

In wrapping up this chapter, it helps to sort out our thinking and ask whether we concede God as the initiator of life. From there, if we examine Jesus Christ and His claims, a whole new world can open up for us. When we consider Christ, we must consider that God incarnate has come to communicate with us.

Summing up this issue of evolution, there are two extremes. First is the assumption that evolution has been proved without doubt and that anyone with a brain in his or her head must accept it. The second is the notion that evolution is "only a theory," with little evidence for it. We reiterate that the so-called conflicts of science and the Bible are often conflicts between interpretations of the facts and reality.

J.P. Moreland describes: "The presupposition one brings to the facts, rather than the facts themselves, determines one's conclusion. For instance, one might be told that his wife was seen riding around town with another man. Knowing his wife, he draws a different conclusion from this fact than does the town gossip. The different conclusions result, not from different facts, but from different presuppositions brought to the fact."[24]

In everything we read and in everything we hear, let's ask, "What is this person's presupposition?" so that we may interpret conclusions in this light. There is generally no such thing as total objectivity.

Many have found that God can act in miraculous ways, and in the past He often chose to. The Bible discloses that He was involved in His original creation and continues in a wise and purposeful relationship with it. While there are problems for which there is as yet no clear explanation, science and Scripture have signs of becoming strong allies.

Why Does God Allow Suffering and Evil?

W hy God allows suffering and evil in our world is one of the most pressing questions of our time. More pressing than the question of miracles or the question concerning science and the Bible is the poignant problem of why seemingly innocent people suffer, why babies are born blind, or why a promising life is snuffed out when it is on the rise. Why are there wars in which thousands of civilians are killed, children are burned beyond recognition, and many are maimed for life?

Seemingly the answer to this question pinpoints two sides of the dilemma for Christians:

- God is *all-powerful* but *not* all-good, and therefore He doesn't want to stop evil.
- God is *all-good* but *unable* to stop evil, and therefore He is not all-powerful.

By responding to this question either way, the general tendency is to blame God for suffering and evil and thus pass all responsibility for them to Him.

No Easy Answers

This profound question is not one that can be treated lightly or in a dogmatic fashion. Let's go back and recall what happened when God created Adam and Eve; He created them perfect. They were not created evil. As human beings, however, Adam and Eve did have the ability to obey or disobey God. Had they obeyed God, there would never have been a problem. They would have lived an unending life of blissful fellowship with God and enjoyment of Him and His creation. This is what

> **"As sure as I lived, I knew that I possessed a will . . . nobody else was making the choice for me."**
> *Augustine of Hippo*

God had intended for them when He created them. In fact, however, they rebelled against God when they ate the forbidden fruit.

From that time on, every one of us has ratified that rebellion and taken the same route. "Therefore," declared the Apostle Paul, "just as sin entered the world through one man, and death through sin, and in this way death came to all men, because all sinned" (Rom. 5:12). It is people who are responsible for sin—not God.

But many ask, "Why didn't God make us so we couldn't sin?" To be sure, God could have. But let's remember that if He had done so we would no longer be human beings; we would be machines, mere puppets on a string. How would you like to be married to a mechanical doll? Every morning and every night you could pull the string and get the beautiful words, "I love you." But who would want that? There really would never be any love because true love is voluntary. Our choices are voluntary. God could have made us like robots, but we would have ceased to be human. Would you like to be a robot? Few of us would honestly answer yes. God apparently thought it worth the risk of creating us as we are and this is the reality we face.

God Could Have Stamped Out Evil!

Jeremiah reminds us, "Because of the Lord's great love we are not consumed, for his compassions never fail" (Lam. 3:22). A time is coming when God *will* stamp out evil in the world. The Devil and all his works will come under eternal judgment. In the meantime, God's unchanging love and grace prevail, and His marvelous offer of mercy and pardon is still open to everyone.

If God were to stamp out evil today, He would do a complete job. We want Him to stop war but stay remote from us. If God were to remove evil from the universe, His action would be complete and would have to include our lies and personal impurities, our lack of love and our failure to do good. Suppose God were to decree that tonight all evil would be removed from the universe—who of us would still be here after midnight?

The Bible tells us the sobering truth by explaining: Sin has been passed on to all humankind through Adam and Eve's choice, and each of us has chosen to follow. From birth we begin by asserting, "No." The sin of Adam and Eve separated them from the close relationship they had with God, and it does likewise for us. The perfect holiness of God can allow no less than separation. It is the consequence of our choices.

God's Ultimate Solution

In this dismal situation, the loving God has done the most dramatic, costly, and effective thing possible by sending His Son to die on our behalf. It is possible for people to escape God's inevitable judgment on sin and evil. It's also possible to have its power broken by entering into a personal relationship with the Lord Jesus Christ. The ultimate answer to the problem of evil, at the personal level, is found in the sacrificial death of Jesus Christ.

To speculate about the origin of evil is endless. No one has the full answer. It belongs in the category of "the secret things [that] belong to the Lord our God" (Deut. 29:29).

Hugh Evan Hopkins observes:

The problem (of evil) arises largely from the belief that a good God would reward each man according to his deeds and that an almighty God would have no difficulty in carrying this out. The fact that rewards and punishments, in the way of happiness and discomfort, appear to be haphazardly distributed in this life drives many to question either the goodness of God or his power.[1]

But would God be good if He were to deal with each person exactly according to his or her behavior? Consider what this would mean in your own life! The whole of the Gospel as previewed in the Old Testament and broadcast in stereo in the New Testament is that God's goodness consists not only in His justice but also in His love, mercy, and kindness. How thankful everyone should be that "he does not treat us as our sins deserve or repay us according to our iniquities. For as high as the heavens are above the earth, so great is his love for those who fear him" (Ps. 103:10-11).

Such a concept of the goodness of God is also based on the faulty assumption that happiness is the greatest good in life. Happiness is usually thought of in terms of comfort. True, genuine, deep-seated happiness, however, is something much more profound than the ephemeral, fleeting enjoyment of the moment. And true happiness is not precluded by suffering. Sometimes, in His infinite wisdom, God knows that there are things to be accomplished in our character that can be brought about only through suffering. To shield us from this suffering would be to rob us of a greater good. "One reason sin flourishes is that it is treated like a cream puff instead of a rattlesnake."[2]

Exact Reward Concept

The Apostle Peter referred to this issue of suffering as a believer when he said, "And the God of all grace, who called you to his eternal glory in Christ, after you have suffered a little while, will himself restore you and make you strong, firm and steadfast" (1 Peter 5:10).

To see the logical consequence of the exact reward concept, coined by John Stuart Mill, we need only turn to Hinduism. The law of karma says that what is experienced today is the result of the actions of a previous life. Blindness, poverty, hunger, physical deformity, isolation, and other social agonies are all the outworking of punishment for evil deeds carried out in a previous existence.

It would follow that any attempt to alleviate such pain and misery would be an interference with the law of karma. This concept is one reason why the Hindus did so little for so long for their unfortunates. Some enlightened Hindus today are talking about and working toward social progress and change, but they have not yet reconciled this new concept with the ancient doctrine of karma, which is basic to Hindu thought and life.

This concept of karma, however, does serve as a neat, simple, clearly understood explanation of suffering: All suffering is the result of previous evil-doing. Dr. Douglas Groothuis asks a penetrating question: If a child dying of leukemia is suffering because she slaughtered innocent people in a former life, she would neither be aware of her previous transgression nor could she learn from it in her present condition.

> **Sin and suffering flourish when sin is treated like a cream puff instead of a rattlesnake.**

But does Christianity also hold that suffering is punishment from God? In the minds of many, it certainly does. "What did I do to deserve this?" is often the first question on the lips of a sufferer. And the conviction of friends, expressed or unexpressed, frequently operates on this same assumption. The classic treatment of the problem of suffering and evil is in the Book of Job, which shows how Job's friends accepted and asserted this cruel assumption. Indeed, it compounded his already staggering pain.

It is clear from the teaching of both the Old and the New Testaments that suffering may be the judgment of God, but that there are many instances when it is totally unrelated to personal wrongdoing. Therefore, an automatic assumption of guilt and consequent punishment is totally unwarranted.

God is not a sentimental grandfather in the sky with a boys-will-be-boys attitude. "A man reaps what he sows" (Gal. 6:7) is a solemn warning to any who would tweak God's nose in arrogant presumption.

That there may be a connection between suffering and sin is evident, but that it is not always so is abundantly clear. We have the unambiguous word of Jesus Himself on the subject. The disciples apparently adhered to the direct retribution theory of suffering. One day when they saw a man who had been blind from birth, they wanted to know who had sinned to cause his blindness—the man or his parents. Jesus made it clear that neither was responsible for his condition, "but this happened so that the work of God might be displayed in his life" (John 9:3).

On receiving word of some Galileans whom Pilate had slaughtered, Jesus went out of His way to point out that they were not greater sinners than other Galileans. He said that the eighteen people who had been killed when the tower of Siloam fell on them were not greater sinners than others in Jerusalem. From both incidents Jesus made the point, "Unless you repent, you too will all perish" (Luke 13:3).

Clearly, then, we are jumping the gun if we automatically assume, either in our own case or in that of another, that the explanation for any given tragedy or suffering is the judgment of God. Furthermore, as Hopkins observes, it seems clear from biblical examples that if one's troubles are the just rewards of misdeeds, the sufferer is never left in any doubt when his or her trouble is a punishment.

Judgment Preceded by Warning

One of the profound truths of the whole of Scripture is that God's warning precedes His judgment. Throughout the Old Testament, we have the repeated pleadings of God and warning of judgment. Only after warning is persistently ignored and rejected does judgment come. God's poignant words from the mouth of His prophet Ezekiel are an example: "I take no pleasure in the death of the wicked, but rather that they turn from their ways and live. Turn! Turn from your evil ways! Why will you die, O house of Israel?" (Ezek. 33:11)

The same theme continues in the New Testament. What more moving picture of God's love and long-suffering is there than when Jesus wept over Jerusalem: "I have longed to gather your children together," He said, "as a hen gathers her chicks under her wings, but you were not willing" (Matt. 23:37). And we have the clear word of Peter that God does not want "anyone to perish, but everyone to come to repentance" (2 Peter 3:9).

When someone asks, "How could a good God send people to hell?" we should point out that, in a sense, God sends no one to hell. We send ourselves. God has done all that is necessary for us to be forgiven, redeemed, cleansed, and made fit for heaven. All that remains is for us to receive this gift. If we refuse it, God has no option but to give us our choice. Heaven, for the person who does not want to be there, would be hell.

Though the judgment of God sometimes explains suffering, there are several other possibilities to consider. People, as we saw earlier, were responsible for the coming of sin and death into the world. We must not forget that humankind's wrongdoing is also responsible for a great deal of misery and suffering in the world today. Negligence in the construction of a building has sometimes resulted in its collapse in a storm with consequent death and injury. How many lives have been snuffed out as a result of drunken driving? The cheating, lying, stealing, and selfishness that are characteristic of our society today all reap a bitter harvest of suffering. But we can hardly blame God for it! Think of all the misery that has its origin in the wrongdoing of human beings; it is remarkable how much suffering is accounted for in this way.

Does the Devil Exist?

But we are not alone on this planet. By divine revelation we know of the presence of an "enemy," the Devil. We are told that he appears in various forms which he deems appropriate to each occasion. He may appear as an angel of light or as a roaring lion, depending on the circumstances and his purposes. His name is Satan. It was he whom God allowed to cause Job to suffer (Job 1:6-12). In the Parable of the Tares, Jesus described the destruction of a farmer's harvest by saying, "An enemy did this" (Matt. 13:28).

Satan finds great pleasure in ruining God's creation and causing misery and suffering among people. God allows him limited power, but through the power of Jesus Christ, we have authority over Satan's power. "Resist the devil, and he will flee from you" (James 4:7), we are assured. Nevertheless, Satan accounts for some of the disease and suffering in the world today.

In answer to the question of why God allows Satan's power to bring suffering, we can learn from Daniel Defoe's eighteenth-century classic, *Robinson Crusoe*, in which the following dialogue takes place:

"Well," says Friday, "you say God is so strong, so great; has he not as much strong, as much might as the devil?"

"Yes, yes," says I; "Friday, God is much stronger than the devil."

"But if God much strong, much might as the devil why God no kill the devil so make him no more do wicked?"

"You may as well ask," answers Crusoe reflectively, "why does

God *not* kill you and me when we do wicked things that offend him?"

God Feels Our Suffering

In considering pain and suffering, whether physical or mental, another important consideration must be kept in mind. God is not a distant, aloof, impervious potentate, far removed from His people and their sufferings. He not only is aware of human suffering—He feels it.

No pain or suffering has ever come to us that has not first passed through the heart and hand of God. However greatly we may suffer, it is well to remember that God is the great sufferer. Comforting are the words of Isaiah the prophet, foretelling the agony of Jesus Christ: "He was despised and rejected by men, a man of sorrows, and familiar with suffering" (Isa. 53:3). Another writer reminds us, "Because he himself suffered when he was tempted, he is able to help those who are being tempted" (Heb. 2:18). And "We do not have a high priest who is unable to sympathize with our weaknesses, but we have one who has been tempted in every way, just as we are—yet was without sin" (4:15). Moreover, we are not to "grieve the Holy Spirit of God" (Eph. 4:30).

> Isaiah tells us, "In all their distress he [God] too was distressed . . . in his love and mercy he redeemed them; he lifted them up and carried them all the days of old." (60:9)

The problem of evil and suffering has persisted through the ages. With our increased technological know-how, the possibilities for tyranny and inhumanity of every kind have multiplied. There are no easy answers, and we do not have the last word. There are, however, clues.

The Risky Gift of Free Will

• First, evil is a necessary part of free will. J.B. Phillips provides these insights:

Evil is inherent in the risky gift of free will. God could have made us machines but to do so would have robbed us of our precious freedom of choice, and we would have ceased to be human. Exercise of free choice in the direction of evil in what we call the "fall" of man [Adam's sin in the garden of Eden] is the basic reason for evil and suffering in the world. It is man's responsibility, not God's. He could stop it, but in so doing would destroy us all. It is worth noting that the whole point of real Christianity lies not in interference with the human power to choose, but in producing a *willing consent* to choose good rather than evil.[3]

Unless the universe is without significance, the actions of every individual affect others. No one is an island. To have it otherwise would be like playing a game of chess and changing the rules after every move. Life would be meaningless.

• Second, much of the suffering in the world can be traced directly to the evil choices men and women make. This is quite apparent when a bank robber kills someone. Sometimes it is less apparent and more indirect as when crooked decisions are made in government or business that may bring deprivation and suffering to many people unknown to those who make the decisions. Even the results of natural disasters are sometimes compounded by people's culpability in refusing to heed warnings of their coming.

• Third, some but not all suffering is allowed by God as judgment and punishment. This is a possibility that must always be considered. God usually allows such suffering with a view to restoration of a person or a people and character formation, and those who suffer as a result of their misdeeds usually know it (Heb. 12:7-8, 11).

• Fourth, God has a vengeful and implacable enemy in Satan, who was defeated at the cross but is free to work his evil deeds until the final judgment. That there is in the world a force of evil stronger than human beings is clear from revelation and from experience.

• Fifth, God Himself is the great sufferer and has fully met the problem of evil in the gift of His own Son at infinite cost and suffering to Himself. The consequence of evil for eternity is forever removed as we embrace

Jesus Christ as our Savior and Lord. Our sin is forgiven and we receive new life and power to choose what is God's best way for us. He directs us and strengthens us and forms us to be more like Jesus Christ in our character.

Greatest Test of Faith

Perhaps the greatest test of faith for the Christian today is to believe that God is good. There is much in our lives and culture that, taken in isolation, suggests the contrary. Theologian Helmut Thielecke

> God's pledge is not that suffering will never afflict us, but that it will never separate us from His love.

points out that a fabric viewed through a magnifying glass is clear in the middle and blurred at the edges. Because of what we see in the middle, we know for certain the edges are clear. Life, he says, is like viewing a fabric.

Around the many edges of our lives, much is blurred, for we do not understand many of its events and circumstances. But they can be interpreted rightly by the clarity we see in the center—the cross of Christ. We are not left to guess about the goodness of God from isolated bits of data. He has clearly revealed His character and dramatically demonstrated it to us in the cross. "He who did not spare his own Son, but gave him up for us all—how will he not also, along with him, graciously give us all things?" (Rom. 8:32)

God never asks us to understand, but just to trust Him in the same way we ask our child to trust our love and care when we take him or her to a doctor. Peace comes when we recognize in this life we do not have the full picture. Yet we do have enough to show us that the edges will be great.

We can affirm, with calm relief and joy, "that in all things God works for the good of those who love him" (v. 28).

At times it is our reaction to suffering, rather than the suffering itself, that determines whether the experience is one of blessing or of blight. The same sun melts the butter and hardens the clay.

When by God's grace we can view all of life through the lens of faith in God's love, we can affirm with Habakkuk: "Though the fig tree does not bud and there are no grapes on the vines, though the olive crop fails and the fields produce no food, though there are no sheep in the pen and no cattle in the stalls, yet I will rejoice in the Lord, I will be joyful in God my Savior" (Hab. 3:17-18).

Does Christianity Differ from Other World Religions?

How Christianity differs significantly from other religions is a subject often discussed in our shrinking modern world. We see a mixture of cultures, nations, races, and religions on a scale unprecedented in history. We are no more than twenty-four hours to any spot on earth from our local airports. Television brings into our living rooms the Dalai Lama seen in Pakistan, Muslims bowing in Iran, and racial and religious wars in Africa.

Over 563,000 students and postdoctoral scholars from over 212 countries came to the United States in the academic year 1996–97 to study in more than 2,428 colleges and universities in every one of the fifty states.[1] Brightly colored saris on graceful Indian women and striking turbans on erect Sikhs are familiar sights in local malls and college towns. In addition, thousands of foreign diplomats, businesspeople, and tourists come to North America every year.

These newcomers find their way into parent-teacher organization meetings, service clubs, and churches to speak on their cultural and religious backgrounds. They are sincere, educated, and intelligent. Moreover, they are often interested in learning about Christianity, and at the same time we can learn from them.

Is Christianity Unique?

As we have contact with these friends from overseas, their religious beliefs naturally raise questions for all of us as to whether Christianity is true or false. Is it unique among world religions? Or is it simply a variation on a basic theme running through all religions? To put it another way, Does not the sincere Muslim, Buddhist, or Hindu worship the same God as we do, but under a different name? Or, quite bluntly, Is Jesus Christ the only way to God?

When the Bible asserts that Jesus Christ is the only way to God and that apart from Him there is no salvation, this belief can leave the impression Christians are bigoted and narrow-minded. Or worse, people may assume that Christians think they are better than anyone else. It may seem to them that Christians have their own private club for bigots, like a fraternity with a racial segregation clause. Discussions on religion can have a potentially explosive element which could defeat any amicable interchange. Both sides can be thinking, "Why aren't you normal like me?" as Bill Hybels has suggested.

Meanwhile, it's common to hear statements like, "Let everyone just believe in God"; "Why bring Jesus Christ into it?"; "Agree on God and that's enough." But can Christianity blend in with other religions and stop being exclusive?

The Crux of the Message

Fundamentally, for the Christian, it is impossible to be theologically inclusive. The cornerstone of the Christian message is Jesus Christ—God come to earth. Without this basis, every other part of the Christian faith lacks meaning. In fact, a multitude of verses in the New Testament assert this basic belief. I'll quote three of them here: *"Salvation is found in no one else, for there is no other name under heaven given to men by which we must be saved"* (Acts 4:12, italics added). The Apostle John said, "No one has ever seen God, but *God the One and Only, who is at the Father's side, has made him known*" (John 1:18, italics added). Jesus made His summary statement, "*I am the way and the truth and the life. No one comes to the Father except through me*" (14:6, italics added).

Christians believe this, not because they have made it their rule, but because Jesus Christ and the Bible, their source, state it. In fact, this core message is woven through both the Old and New Testaments. A Christian is not giving his or her own bias but is explaining the biblical facts.

If we should say we would like to change this truth and vote in something more inclusive, here is our dilemma. We would be changing

> **The uniqueness of Christ is threefold:**
>
> **His incarnation, God came to earth.**
>
> **He died, "the just One for the unjust," on the cross.**
>
> **He rose again to authenticate who He was and why He came.**

something that is not humanly changeable. It is fixed and is either completely true or completely false. It is "true-truth," as Francis Schaeffer stated it.

• There are some laws or truths *we could change*. For instance, the penalty for driving through a stoplight is determined by society's vote. It is not inherent in the act itself. The penalty, likewise, could be set at fifty dollars or at ten dollars, or the law could be abolished completely.

• Other laws, like gravity, are irrevocable truths *we cannot change*. They are not socially determined no matter what the opinion polls and culture say. Truth is solid, fixed, and certain. The penalty for violation is not socially determined. People could vote to unanimously suspend the law of gravity for an hour, but no one in his or her right mind would jump off the roof of a skyscraper to test it! No, the penalty for violating gravity is inherent in the act itself, and the person who violated it would be picked up with a blotter despite the unanimous resolution!

• As there are inherent physical laws, so there are *inherent spiritual laws.* One of them is God's initiative when He revealed Himself in Jesus Christ's coming to earth. Another is Christ's death as the route to forgiveness of sins and the beginning of a one-on-one relationship with God. To talk about the exclusiveness of Christ, a Christian is not assuming a superior posture in any way. There is no room for arrogance. Rather, it is a person whose life has been touched by God's intervention and grace. D.T. Niles describes Christians telling their personal stories with: "It is just one beggar telling another beggar where to find food."

Is Sincerity Enough?

Having seen that spiritual truth is not arrived at by a majority vote, a general consideration of truth does help. To begin with, *sincerely believing something* does not make it true, as anyone will testify who has ever picked a wrong bottle out of a medicine cabinet in the dark. We've previously said faith is no more valid than the object in which it is placed. It doesn't matter how sincere or how intense the faith. A nurse put carbolic acid in the eyes of a newborn baby, sincerely thinking she was applying silver nitrate. Her sincerity did not save the baby from blindness.

These same principles apply to spiritual things. *Believing something doesn't make it true any more than failing to believe truth makes it false.* Facts are facts, regardless of people's attitudes toward them. In religious matters, the basic question is always, Is it true?

Ravi Zacharias gives helpful insight on the laws of logic. First, there is the *either/or principle,* the law of noncontradiction. Either Jesus Christ is God *or* not God: true *or* not true. If Jesus Christ is God, Brahma or one of the 330 million gods cannot be true God too. If Jesus Christ was the author of creation, as the Bible teaches, it was not Brahma. It was either one or the other. Think back, the carbolic acid was either poisonous or not!

This logic would be like me saying, "Since there is no bus coming, I will cross the street." But you might say "Since there *is* a bus coming, I will not cross." We would know the truth when I cross the street. One must be true and the other not.

The opposite logic would be the *both/and principle.* This says both Brahma and Jesus are true God, the polytheistic view. Have as many gods as you want is the essence of this view of God.[2]

The application of the *both/and principle* leads to an impasse in our thinking. Consider creation, for instance. Which God or gods created the world? Which God will tell me truth about life? Which one shall I pray to? How do I know which one is good and which one is not? Can there be Jesus and a plethora of other gods?

Take, for instance, the fact of the deity, death, and resurrection of Jesus Christ. Christianity affirms these facts as the heart of its message. Islam, on the other hand, denies the deity, death, and resurrection of Christ. On this very crucial point, one of these mutually contradictory views is *untrue and wrong*. They cannot both be simultaneously true, no matter how sincerely both are believed by any number of people.

A great deal is said about the similarity of world religions. Many Christians naively assume that all world religions are basically the same, that they all make the same claims, and that other religions essentially teach what Christianity teaches but in slightly different terms. It would seem that such an attitude of using the *both/and principle* makes all religions identical. In other words, "both Islam and Christianity are true." Incidentally, faithful followers of the Islamic faith would strongly object to this statement.

The fact is, though there are some similarities between the major world religions, *their differences far outweigh their common elements.*

Is the Golden Rule Enough?

One of the similarities is the belief in the Golden Rule, which is contained in almost every religion. From Confucius' time we have the statement in various forms: Do unto others as we would have others do unto us. This is sometimes assumed to be the essence of Christianity. If all Jesus Christ did was give us the Sermon on the Mount and the Golden Rule, however, He would have actually increased our frustration. Few of us can consistently keep those teachings. Our problem has never been *not knowing what we should do*. Our problem, rather, has been *lacking the power*, the ability, to do what we know is helpful, moral, good, just, honest, kind, and so on.

Jesus Christ not only taught the Golden Rule, but He also came to help us keep it. This is essentially the major distinction between Christianity and other religions. He offers us His power to live as we should, while giving us God's forgiveness as a free gift. He provides us with His "new" life—that is, His own righteousness. We can start over again, for He does something for us we cannot do for ourselves.

Basic Christianity

If this list of God's actions seems too good to be true, a brief look at God's character is our starting point for basic Christianity. In *Becoming a Contagious Christian*, Bill Hybels and Mark Mittelberg explain the three seminal characteristics of God:

> First of all, God is *loving*. Out of His compassion He made us and desires to have a relationship with us. He continues to patiently extend His love to us. Many people prefer to stop here, but there's more that needs to be said. Secondly, you see, God is *holy*. This means that He is absolutely pure and He is separate from everything that is impure.
>
> The third characteristic of God is He is *just*. In other words, He is like a good judge who can't wink at a broken law: rather, He must mete out justice.[3]

The most difficult thing for us to comprehend is God's total separateness from us and our standard of holiness. When we rise in anger over senseless and vicious acts against the helpless, we experience only an inkling of His abhorrence of evil. "He cannot even look at evil," the Bible describes Him. It is God's nature to be righteous and just. God's infinite holiness far exceeds ours, like comparing the difference between the top of the tallest tree as our standard of holiness and the moon as God's standard.

One college graduate told me soberly, "If God grades on the curve, I'll be OK." He felt he was about average in his life and morals. God, to him, was a professor with set guidelines, and he came out average.

To get a brief summary of the heart of biblical Christianity we will look at the most universally quoted verse in the Bible—John 3:16:

• *"God so loved the world."* He loves each one of us whom He created. The phrase "so loved" expresses "more than a mother cares for a child." Indeed, He cares for each of us.

• *"That he gave his one and only Son"*—Jesus Christ—to come to earth, "to rescue us," to be our "truth and life." All of our ethical and moral remedies have failed. We have turned away from God's way, and we need a Savior. This is not man struggling toward God, but God reaching down for us. He knew more rules would not help. Instead, the holy and just God came to earth, and they called Him Jesus, "because he will save his people from their sins" (Matt. 1:21).

- *"That whoever believes in him"*. . . this offer is open to all—anyone who will come to Him He lovingly receives. Whoever says, "Yes, I need You," will know that He answers. He brings divine help and forgiveness. He gives a whole new life and cements a relationship with Himself. Give yourself to Him and you will find your real self, as your Creator intended you to be.

- *"Shall not perish but have eternal life."* He rescues you and "saves" you from "perishing" because of your sins and failures. You will be forgiven, freed from binding habits and from ceaseless waywardness and repetitious guilt. Eternal life is God's life that He gives us. "A new person," the Apostle Paul calls it. Whatever our circumstances, He receives us and gladly rescues us from the seas of uncertainty and emptiness. Imagine life with your hand in His hand each day!

Receiving Him into your life is not a do-it-yourself proposition. It is not saying, "Work hard at it and follow this way and you will gain favor with God." It is not a set of swimming instructions for a drowning man. In Christianity, Jesus Christ Himself comes to be our life Preserver.

A Free Gift

A "life Preserver" is one who jumps in, helps, and saves. Jesus described His coming as "giving his life a ransom for many." This is His free gift to us. He was God-come-to-earth who willingly came alongside us to help. D.T. Niles explains that in other religions people are left to do the best they can, follow the rules, and do "good works." These are all in order to gain their own particular promised goal (and every religion offers some promised utopia and euphoria).

Mark Mittelberg clarifies the dif-

> God became man to turn creatures into sons: not simply to produce better men of the old kind but to produce a new kind of man.

ference between religion and Christianity. "Religion is spelled 'Do,' because it consists of the things people *do* to try to somehow gain God's forgiveness and favor. . . . Thankfully Christianity is spelled differently. It's spelled 'D-O-N-E.'"[4]

We do good deeds, on the other hand, because Jesus became our life Preserver—that is, our Savior. They are an expression of our love and gratitude to Him.

The mystery of God's love and Jesus' coming as our Rescuer is found in His death on the cross. This innocent God-man was cruelly slaughtered for simply admitting He was God come in the flesh. At the cross alone the love and justice of God are bound together. Here all our moral and human failures have been declared forgiven. The cross speaks the message of forgiveness from church towers to jewelry counters: love and justice satisfied.

Apologist William Lane Craig tells a story of three men's reactions when they finally saw Christ's reality.

Three men stood in a crowd before God's throne on the Judgment Day. Each had a score to settle with God. "I was hanged for a crime I didn't commit," complained one man bitterly. "I died from a disease that dragged on for months, leaving me broken in body and spirit," said another. "My son was killed in the prime of life when some drunk behind the wheel jumped the curb and ran him down," muttered the third. Each was angry and anxious to give God a piece of his mind. But when they reached the throne and saw their Judge with His nail-scarred hands and feet and His wounded side, each mouth was stopped. They dropped silently to their knees at the sight of their Savior.[5]

Three Major Religions

From this picture of God's gift, we will briefly contrast three of the major religions of the world. What salvation is and what they are pointing toward are quite different from the picture we have drawn so far.

• In *Buddhism*, for instance, the ultimate goal for the faithful Buddhist is nirvana, or the extinction of desire. According to the Buddha's teaching, all pain and suffering come from desire. If desire can be eradicated by following the Eightfold Path to Enlightenment, one can achieve nirvana, which is the total cessation of one's identity. It is likened to the blowing out of a candle. This is said to happen to life and consciousness when nirvana has been achieved.

• In *Hinduism* the ultimate goal is also nirvana, but the term here has a different meaning. Nirvana is ultimate reunion with Brahman, the all-pervading force of the universe. For many Hindus, Brahman is the chief god in the Hindu pantheon. This experience is likened to the return of a drop of water to the ocean. Individuality is lost in the reunion with God, but without the total annihilation of a person's identity as taught in Buddhist doctrine.

For the devout Hindu, nirvana is achieved through a continuous cycle of birth, life, death, and rebirth. As soon as any animal, insect, or human being dies, that being is immediately reborn in another form. Whether one moves up or down the scale of life depends on the quality of moral life one has lived. If it has been a good life, one moves up the scale with more comfort and less suffering. If one has lived a bad life, one moves down the scale into suffering and poverty. If one has been bad enough, that person is not reborn as a human being at all but as an animal or insect.

This law of reaping in the next life the harvest of one's present life is called the law of karma. It explains why many Hindus will not kill or eat animals, particularly cows, which are sacred to them because their gods have honored these animals. What seems strange, curious, and even illogical to us of the Western world has a clear rationale to the Hindu.

• In *Islam* heaven is thought of as a paradise of pleasure and indulgence. It is achieved by living a life in which, ironically, one abstains from the things with which he or she will be rewarded in paradise. In addition to this abstention, one must follow the Five Pillars of Islam: repeating the creed, making a pilgrimage to Mecca, giving alms to the poor, praying five times daily, and keeping the fast of Ramadan.

Again, there is no possibility of assurance. I have often asked Buddhists, Hindus, and Muslims whether they will achieve nirvana or go to paradise when they die. I have not yet had one reply in the affirmative. Rather, they referred to the imperfection of their lives as being a barrier to either spiritual goal. There is no assurance in their religious systems; because there is no atonement, salvation depends wholly on the individual's gaining enough merit.

Concept of God

Even the fundamental concept of God, on which there is a plea that we should agree, reveals wide divergences. To say that we can unite with all who believe in God, regardless of what this God is called, fails to recognize that the term *God* means nothing apart from the definition given it.

Contrary to popular belief, the Buddha never claimed to be a deity. In fact, he was agnostic about the whole question of whether God even existed. If God existed, the Buddha taught emphatically, he could not help an individual achieve enlightenment. Each person must work this out for himself or herself.

Meanwhile, the traditional Hindu theology is pantheistic. *Pan* means "all" and *theistic* refers to God. Hindus identify God with all things. The concept of *maya* is central to their thinking. Maya is the false dualistic perception of true reality that results from ignorance of the oneness of all things. Brahman is the ultimate reality—the Universal Soul with which individual seekers strive to become one.

In Islam and Judaism we have a God somewhat closer to the Christian concept. Here God is personal and transcendent, or separate from His creation. Surely, we are urged, we may get together with those who believe in God in personal terms.

But as we examine the Muslim concept of God—Allah as he is called in the Koran or Quran—we find he is not the God and Father of Jesus Christ, but rather, as in all other instances, a God of a leader's conjecture. Knowledge of Allah comes from the Koran, which came through Muhammad, who taught that he was the final prophet of Allah.

The picture of God in the Koran is of one who is totally removed from people, one who is capricious in all of his acts, responsible for evil as well as for good, and who is certainly not the God who "so loved the world that he gave his one and only Son." It is a totally distant concept of God that makes the idea of the Incarnation utterly inconceivable to the Muslim. How could their god, so majestic and beyond, have contact with mortal human beings in sin and misery? The death of God the Son on the cross is likewise inconceivable to a Muslim, because this would mean that God was defeated by His creatures, an impossibility to them.

The Jewish God Is Close

The Jewish concept of God is closest of all world religions to the

Christian concept. Isn't the God whom they worship the God of the Old Testament, which we accept? Surely we can get together on this!

Again, however, closer examination shows that most Jews do not admit their God was the Father of Jesus Christ. Some may believe Jesus was a great man, but not their Messiah (Savior). In fact, it was this very issue that precipitated such bitter controversy in Jesus' time. "God we accept," they said to Jesus Christ, "but we do not accept you because as a man you are claiming yourself to be God, which in our view is a clear case of blasphemy."

In a conversation with the Jewish religious leaders, Jesus discussed this question. "God is our Father," they said. Jesus said to them, "If God were your Father, you would love me, for I came from God. . . . He who belongs to God hears what God says. The reason you do not hear is that you do not belong to God" (John 8:42, 47). In even stronger words Jesus said to those Jews who sought His death, "You belong to your father, the devil" (v. 44).

It is quite obvious the Jewish leaders who were critical of Jesus were not sincere seekers. If people are seeking the true God, their sincerity will be evident and their efforts rewarded. Missionary history has numerous examples of those who have been following other gods or an unknown god but who have responded when presented with the truth about Jesus Christ. The message brings home to them that Jesus is the true God, whom they have been seeking.

Jesus Christ Alone Claims Deity

Of the great religious leaders of the world, Christ alone claims deity. It really doesn't matter what one thinks of Muhammad, Buddha, or Confucius as individuals. Their followers emphasize their teachings. Not so with Christ. He made Himself the focal point of His teachings. The central question He put to His listeners was, "Whom do you say that I am?" When asked what doing the works of God involved, Jesus replied, "The work of God is this: to believe in the one he has sent" (John 6:29).

On the question of who and what God is, the nature of salvation and how it is obtained, it is clear that Christianity differs radically from other world religions. We live in an age in which tolerance is a key word. Tolerance, however, must be clearly understood. (Truth, by its very nature, is intolerant of error.) If two plus two is four, the total at the same time cannot be twenty-three. But one is not regarded as intolerant because he or she disagrees with this answer and maintains that the only correct answer is four.

The same principle applies in religious matters. One must be tolerant of other points of view and respect their right to be held and heard. We cannot, however, be forced in the name of tolerance to agree that all points of view are equally valid, including those that are mutually contradictory. This would be nonsense.

The Only Way to God

It is not true that "it doesn't matter what you believe as long as you believe it." Hitler's slaughter of six million Jews was based on a sincere view of racial supremacy, but he was diabolically wrong. What we believe must be true in order to be real. Again, Jesus said, "I am the way and the truth and the life. No one comes to the Father except through me" (John 14:6). If we are to know the true and living God in personal experience, it will be through Jesus Christ.

Is Christian Experience Valid?

Y ou could get the same response from that table lamp if you believed it possessed the same attributes as your God," said the young law student. This articulate skeptic was telling me what thousands feel—that the Christian experience is completely personal and subjective and has no objective, eternal, and universal validity.

The premise behind this notion is that the mind is capable of infinite rationalization. Belief in God is seen as mere wish fulfillment. In adults, it is a throwback to our need for a father image. The assumption, whether expressed or not, is that Christianity is for emotional cripples, who can't make it through life without a crutch.

It is claimed that the Christian conversion is a psychologically induced experience brought about by brainwashing similar to the methods used by both fascists and communists. An evangelist is just a master of psychological manipulation. After pounding away at an audience, he finds that people become putty in his hands. He can get them to do anything if he asks for a decision at the right time and in the right way.

Some critics go further. The Christian experience, they claim, is sometimes exceedingly harmful. More than one student has been packed off to a psychiatrist by nonbelieving parents after he or she has come to a personal faith in Jesus Christ. "Look at all the religious nuts in mental asylums. It's their religion that put them there." Those who feel this way have succumbed to the "common-factor fallacy," pointed out by Anthony Standen. He tells of a man who got drunk each Monday on whiskey and soda water; on Tuesday he got drunk on brandy and soda water; and Wednesday on gin and soda water. What caused the drunkenness? Obviously the common factor, soda water![1]

The Last Stop on the Train

For many, the church is thought of as the last stop on the train before being institutionalized. A careful scrutiny of a truly disoriented person, however, would reveal imbalance and unreality in other areas as well as in his or her religious life. Some of these people do, in fact, need professional care. On the other hand, some emotional problems have sprung from spiritual roots. As these people come into a right relationship with God through Jesus Christ, they find release and healing.

Admittedly, prejudice does exist in some quarters against the validity of the Christian experience, even denying academic degrees if theistic belief is discovered. A friend, studying in one of our best-known universities, was denied a Ph.D. degree in social science. He was told, "Believing what you do about God, you are by definition crazy."

Aggressive skeptics have suggested that all Christian experience can be explained on the basis of conditioned reflexes. In a college you may have studied the experiments of Ivan Pavlov, the famous Russian scientist. He placed measuring devices in a dog's mouth and stomach to determine the production of digestive juices. Then he would bring food to the dog and at the same time ring a bell. After doing this repeatedly over a period of time, Pavlov rang the bell without producing the food and the dog salivated as usual. The inference drawn is that by such repeated conditioning, the mind can be made to produce desired physical reactions. Many skeptics of the Christian faith use this scientific experiment to explain all political, social, and religious conversions.

These are serious, far-reaching charges, and yet some of them have an air of plausibility.

Is the Christian Experience Valid?

At the outset, we must concede the possibility that religious zealots can manipulate human emotions. We admit that some evangelists consciously or unconsciously play on the emotions of their audiences with deathbed stories, histrionic performances, and other manipulative devices.

Jesus cautioned against this type of evangelism, however, when He told a parable about a farmer who sowed seeds in his field. This parable (a story with a deeper meaning) was His way of communicating to others God's good news of hope about Himself to others.

As the farmer worked, seeds fell in various places. The seed represents God's message, and those seeds that fell on the rocky soil refers to God's message being received by some people with immediate joy, but when hard times come, their hopes are dashed, and they turn away from God.

The story is intended to caution us all to let the seed of the Christian message sink deeply into our minds and hearts. Superficial belief when our emotions are high can disappear easily. Life, in general, is solving problems, as we all have discovered. "Not every day is a three-cookie day," as Max Lucado suggests. Emotions are undulant and may even vary with the weather, but Christian truth does not rest on emotional highs. A key is to recognize whether our emotions govern our judgments too strongly.

A Matter of the Will

Dr. Orville S. Walters, a Christian psychiatrist, has pointed out the significance of the will, especially in our faith in God. The will, he says, is like a cart pulled by two horses—the emotions and the intellect. With some people the will is reached more quickly through the emotions. With others it is reached through the mind. But in every case there is no genuine beginning of belief and trust in Jesus Christ unless the will has been involved.[2]

Any attempt to explain all Christian experience on a psychological basis does not fit the facts. Here as in other areas: To describe something is not the same thing as explaining it. God *does respond* to the one who speaks to Him. When we hear of the love of God and the cross of Jesus Christ, it does move our hearts and emotions. The account of the three bitter men in the previous chapter is a graphic illustration of this. They turned from complaining and doubting God's goodness to uninhibited worship.

One evidence that Christianity is true is the reality of the experience of those who embrace Jesus Christ. One of the challenges the psalmist throws out to us when we question is "Taste and see that the Lord is good" (Ps. 34:8). Verify for yourself in the laboratory of life the hypothesis that Jesus Christ is the living Son of God. The Christian experience is one unmistakable confirmation of faith in Christ. When we couple the Christian experience with its twin truth of God's objective revelation, we are assured of the trustworthiness of God's message.

A Conditioned Reflex?

Another objection I've heard is that the Christian experience is merely a conditioned reflex—similar, in fact, to other creatures. William Sargant wrote a widely influential book called *Battle for the Mind* in which he discussed whether the comparison between people and animals is a strictly legitimate one.

Dr. D. Martyn Lloyd-Jones answered Sargant's question by stating that a human being has reason, a critical faculty, and powers of self-analysis, self-contemplation, and self-criticism that make him or her quite different from animals. "In other words, the comparison is only valid at times (like war) when what differentiates man has been knocked out of action and a man, because of terrible stress, has been reduced for the time being to the level of an animal."[3]

In addition, if we are only creatures of conditioned reflexes, then this must also explain acts of great heroism and self-sacrifice in which human beings have taken pride. Such acts must be nothing but responses to a given stimulus at a given point. Taken to its logical conclusion, a deterministic view of human behavior eliminates moral responsibility. The little girl who said, "It ain't my fault; it's my glands," would be right. It is significant, however, that those holding a deterministic point of view philosophically tend to operate on a different basis in daily life; like anyone else, they want a murderer arrested promptly!

Conditioned reflex does not explain the vast number of people who tell of their undeniable Christian experience. Thousands raised in Christian homes unfortunately never become Christians while thousands of other people sincerely trust Christ. The experience cannot be explained away exclusively on the basis of a person's background.

Personal faith in Christ is the only door to becoming a Christian, but the roads that lead to that door are almost as many as the number who enter it. I have known persons who became Christians the first time they heard the Gospel message. By contrast, it has been documented that in political brainwashing, as with Pavlov's experiments, the stimulus must be applied consistently and repeatedly in order to achieve the desired result.

Those who have become Christians out of every conceivable religious background or out of no background at all uniformly testify to a personal inner confirmation. For them, wholehearted commitment to Jesus Christ brought a confirming, subjective experience. Visibly changed lives confirms this experience. Thousands of stories could be told as well as read about.

Positive thinking, any more than a table lamp, cannot be responsible for such results. What occurs in a soul transformed by God is far more substantial than either what positive thinking or a table lamp can produce. Incidentally, the law student referred to at the beginning of this chapter committed his life to Jesus Christ in the course of the week's lectures that followed.

Victims of Autohypnosis?

Yet how do we know when we become Christians that we are not victims of autohypnosis? How do we know we are not just whistling in the dark? Subjective experience, as such, does not prove anything. Many have claimed an experience the reality of which one may legitimately question. There must be more than experience on which to base our conviction. Otherwise, we are in a terrible fix.

For instance, suppose a man with a fried egg over his left ear came through the door of a church. "Oh," exclaims this man, who is glowing with happiness, "this egg really gives me joy, peace, purpose in life, forgiveness of sins, and strength for living!" What would you say to him? You can't tell him he hasn't experienced these things. One of the powers of professed personal experience is that it can't be argued. The blind man whom Jesus healed couldn't answer many of the questions put to him, but he was sure of the fact that now he could see (see John 9). His testimony was eloquent in its power.

Nevertheless, what would we ask our friend with the fried egg on his ear? We would not honestly remark, "Oh, that's nice!"

• First, we must ask this important question: *"Who else has had the same experience* with the fried egg?" Presumably our friend would be hard put to produce others. The late Harry Ironside was preaching some years ago when a heckler shouted, "Atheism has done more for the world than Christianity!"

"Very well," said Ironside, "tomorrow night you bring a hundred men whose lives have been changed for the better by atheism, and I'll bring a hundred who have been transformed by Christ."

Needless to say, his heckler friend did not appear the next night. With Christianity, there are hundreds from every race, every country, and every walk of life who bear testimony to an experience through Jesus Christ.

• Next, we must ask these questions: "What *objective reality* does our friend with the fried egg have? What objective reality *outside of himself* is his internal subjective experience tied to? How does he know he is not a victim of autohypnosis?" Doubtless, he will not have much to say. In Christianity our personal subjective experience is tied into the objective historical fact of the resurrection of Jesus Christ. If Christ did not rise from the dead, we would not and cannot experience Him. It's because He rose from the dead and is living today that we can actually know Him.

Objective Historical Fact

Christian experience is not induced by belief in unrealities. It is not like the fraternity boy who died of fright when he was tied to a railroad track one night during hazing. He was told that a train would be coming in five minutes. He was not told that the train would pass on a parallel track. He thought there was only one track. When he heard the train approaching, he suffered heart failure. With Christianity, nothing happens if there is no one out there.

Indisputably, Jesus Christ is really there, not as a coach in the bleachers or a distant relative we never see. He is alive and He is near. All the possibilities of the divine living Creator living within us are realizable. He came to earth specifically to make that connection. We were created to be directed and supported by Him, "to walk with him," as the Bible expresses it. It is a recorded fact that Jesus Christ lived on earth and a historical fact that He rose from the dead. Our personal subjective experience is based on these objective truths.

J.B. Phillips makes an observation about people who are suffering beyond their own capabilities to endure, and how they have drawn upon the power of Jesus Christ in such situations:

> I know perfectly well that I am merely describing subjective phenomena. But the whole point is that . . . I have observed results . . . courage, faith, hope, joy and patience, for instance. . . . The man who wants everything proved by scientific means is quite right in his insistence on "laboratory conditions" if he is investigating, shall we say, water-divining, clairvoyance or telekinesis.
>
> There can be no such thing as "laboratory conditions" for investigating the realm of the human spirit unless it can be seen that the "laboratory conditions" are in fact human life itself. A man can only exhibit objectively a change in his own disposition, a faith which directs his life—*in the actual business of living.*[4]

Rich or poor, high or low, our needs are similar. Ravi Zacharias tells of an interview that TV host David Frost conducted with multimillionaire Ted Turner. When unexpectedly asked if there was anything in his life he regretted, a sudden melancholic expression came on Turner's face. Somberly he answered, "Yes, the way I treated my first wife."[5]

It is in the everyday "human life" environment where deep character changes, attitudes, and other personal relationships cry for help. And this is exactly where we can know the subjective presence of God's Son demonstrated. It is an objective reality.

Purpose and Direction

Jesus Christ gives purpose and direction to life. "I am the light of the world," He said. "Whoever follows me will never walk in darkness, but will have the light of life" (John 8:12). Many are in the dark about the purpose of life in general and about their own lives in particular. They are groping around the room of life looking for the light switch. Anyone who has ever been in a dark, unfamiliar room knows this feeling of insecurity. When the light goes on, however, a feeling of security results. And so it is when one steps from darkness into the light of life in Jesus Christ.

God in Christ gives our lives cosmic purpose, tying us in with His purpose for history and eternity. What we do each day is valued by Him. A Christian lives not only for time but also for eternity. Even daily routine is transformed when we live the whole of our lives for God's purpose and obey the admonition: "Whether you eat or drink or whatever you do, do it all for the glory of God" (1 Cor. 10:31). It is also an unending, eternal purpose. Without faith in God temporary purposes such as family, career, and money occupy us and give limited satisfaction. These, at best, are transient and may fail with a change in circumstances.

To the postmodern world where empirical evidence is asked for, Jesus Christ stands unchanging. While existentialist philosophers declare life meaningless and absurd, nothing could have more power and meaning than this verifiable claim of Christ.

We Have Been Made for God

The late psychologist Carl Gustav Jung said, "The central neurosis of our time is emptiness." When we do not have money, fame, success, power, and other externals, we think we'll achieve final happiness after we attain them. Many testify to the disillusionment experienced when they have achieved these things, and then the realization sets in that one is still the same miserable person. The human spirit can never be satisfied "by bread alone"—that is, with material things. We have been made for God and can find rest only in Him.

An automobile, however shiny, high-powered, and full of equipment, will not run on water. It was made to run only on gasoline. So people can find fulfillment only in God. We were made this way by God Himself. Christian experience offers this fulfillment in a personal relationship with Jesus Christ. He said, *"I am the bread of life.* He who comes to me will never go hungry, and he who believes in me will never be thirsty" (John 6:35, italics added). When individuals experience Christ, they come to an inner contentment, joy, and spiritual refreshment that enables them to transcend circumstances. It was this reality that enabled Paul to say, "I have learned to be content whatever the circumstances" (Phil. 4:11). This supernatural reality enables Christians to rejoice in the middle of difficult circumstances.

Our Quest Is for Peace

"Peace in our time" expresses the longing of each of us as our own mountain of challenges stares us in the face. When we observe the international scene, we hope against hope that the current brushfire wars will not erupt into more bombings from more hidden enemies.

Peace is the quest of every human heart. If it could be bought, people would pay millions for it. The skyrocketing sales of books dealing with peace of mind and soul testify that they have touched a resonant chord in many lives. Psychiatrists' offices are jammed.

Jesus said, "*Come to me, all you who are weary and burdened, and I will give you rest*" (Matt. 11:28, italics added). Christ alone gives peace that passes understanding, a peace the world cannot give or take away. It is very moving to hear the testimony of those who have restlessly searched for years and have finally found peace in Christ. We need not succumb to the current temptation of drugs, alcohol, and sexual obsession, or any other form of escape in the vain hope of gaining the peace that is in Christ alone. "He himself is our peace" (Eph. 2:14).

A Radical Power Needed

Today's society is experiencing a profound power failure—a moral power failure. Parents know what is right for themselves and their children, but for lack of backbone they find it easier to go along with the crowd. Children readily pick up this attitude. The result is rapid deterioration of the moral fabric of our society. Merely to give good advice to either the old or young is like putting iodine on cancer. What is needed is radical power.

Christianity is not putting new clothes on a person, but putting a new person into the clothes. Jesus Christ said, "I have come that they may have life, and have it to the full" (John 10:10). He offers us His power. Not only is there power and freedom from things like alcohol and drugs, but also power to forgive those who have wronged us, to resist temptation, and to love the unlovely. Newborn people have new appetites, new desires, and new loves. They are, in fact, "new creation[s]" (2 Cor. 5:17). New believers in Jesus Christ, in reality, have literally come from spiritual death to spiritual life.

Problems of Guilt and Loneliness Solved

The Christian experience solves the guilt problem. Every normal person feels guilt. The guilt complex is an irrational feeling that has no basis in fact. But guilt felt over something done wrong in violation of an inherent moral law is normal. The absence of any guilt feeling is abnormal. A

> In the Spring term of university I gave in, and admitted that God was God and knelt and prayed; perhaps, that night, the most dejected and reluctant convert in all England. I did not then see what is now the most shining and obvious thing; the Divine humility which will accept a convert even on such terms. The Prodigal Son at least walked home on his own feet. But who can duly adore that Love [of a Divine God] which will open the high gates to a prodigal who is brought in kicking, struggling, resentful, and darting his eyes in every direction for a chance of escape? But who can plumb the depth of the divine mercy? The hardness of God is kinder than the softness of men, and His compulsion is our liberation.
>
> C.S. Lewis, *Surprised by Joy*

person who feels nothing after deliberately killing or hurting an innocent person is abnormal. Guilt must not be rationalized away. In Christ, there is an objective basis for forgiveness. Christ died for our sins; the sentence of death that belonged to us has been taken by Him. *"Therefore, there is now no condemnation for those who are in Christ Jesus"* (Rom. 8:1, italics added). Forgiveness at the personal level is a reality.

Christianity also speaks to people's loneliness, which is compellingly characteristic of modern society. It is ironic that in a period of population explosion people are more lonely than ever. Christ is the Good Shepherd (John 10:14), who will never leave us nor forsake us. And He introduces us into a caring, worldwide family.

New Faith Brings New Life

Finally, in recognizing the validity of the Christian experience, we gradually realize that a psychological description of it is valid as far as it goes. Indeed, it is only a description, not a cause. A person who comes to Jesus

Christ and puts his or her life into His hands is "born anew" or "born of God." He or she has God's Spirit, a new spiritual life within. This new life is likened to natural birth when a newborn baby will come alive, do new things, and learn new things. There are a number of descriptions of "born anew" in the New Testament, such as the following:

- "Everyone who believes that Jesus is the Christ is born of God" (1 John 5:1).
- "You have been born again, not of perishable seed, but of imperishable, through the living and enduring word of God" (1 Peter 1:23).
- "Therefore, if anyone is in Christ, he is a new creation" (2 Cor. 5:17).

The experience of "new life," I hope, will be the culmination of our examining the twelve questions discussed in this book and the rational basis for WHY we believe. Knowing answers does give satisfaction to our minds.

The next step is determining our own status with God, our magnificent Creator, and our individual relationship with Him. You may have already made connection with Him and His offer of "new life." Or you may need to take the next step, deciding to take action and to personally seek Him. Jesus sums up His coming with "I am the gate [likened to a sheep gate]; whoever enters through me will be saved [born anew]" (John 10:9).

Have You Ever Personally Trusted Jesus Christ, or Are You Still on the Way?

A young man sat in our living room and logically threw some hardball questions at me that bothered him about God and the Christian faith. We talked a long while until I finally asked him the above question, had he ever personally put his life and trust in Jesus Christ. I will never forget his reply. Very sincerely he said, "I'm stuck between the screen door and the real door."

The whole issue could not have been expressed more clearly. Many are in the same place . . . still outside, but deep down wanting to get in. The good news that day for both him and me was that he decided he wanted to pray directly to God "in Jesus' name," as he put it. This was something he had never done before.

Bottom-line ingredients were in his prayer. He said:

"*First*, I know I need You, God, in my life. My sins are big and I need to be forgiven.

"*Second*, I ask You, God, through Jesus Christ, to guide my life, make it new, and lead me in all the decisions I make."

Then, he spontaneously poured out some of his inner battles—all with a kind of hope for freedom. At the end of his prayer, he whispered to the Lord, "Thanks."

He went through the door. And Jesus Christ was waiting for him. Incredibly, God is waiting for each of us.

Endnotes

Chapter 1

1. C.S. Lewis, *Mere Christianity* (New York: Macmillan, 1943), p. 24.

2. R.C. Sproul, *Knowing Scripture* (Downers Grove, Ill.: InterVarsity Press, 1977), p. 17.

3. Antony Flew, "Theology and Falsification," in *New Essays in Philosophical Theology*, eds. Antony Flew and Alasdair MacIntyre (London: SCM Press, 1955), n.p.

4. On the issue of theological verification, see John W. Montgomery, "Inspiration and Inerrancy: A New Departure," *Evangelical Theological Society Bulletin* 8 (Spring 1956): 45-75.

5. Bill Hybels, *The God You're Looking For* (Nashville: Thomas Nelson, 1997), p. 7.

6. Stephen Hawking, *A Brief History of Time* (New York: Bantam, 1988), p. 175.

7. C.S. Lewis, *The Quotable Lewis* (Wheaton, Ill.: Tyndale House Publishers, 1989), p. 229.

8. C.S. Lewis, *God in the Dock* (Grand Rapids, Mich.: Eerdmans, 1970), pp. 108-9, 112.

Chapter 2

1. Mortimer Adler, *Great Books of the Western World*, ed. Robert Maynard Hutchins, vol. 2 (Chicago: Encyclopaedia Britannica, 1952), p. 561.

2. Samuel Zwemer, *The Origin of Religion* (Neptune, N.J.: Loizeaux Brothers, 1945), n.p.

3. R.C. Sproul, *Reason to Believe* (Grand Rapids, Mich.: Zondervan, 1978), p. 112.

4. Lincoln Barnett, *The Universe and Dr. Einstein* (New York: Bantam, 1974), p. 95.

5. Fred Hoyle, *The Intelligent Universe* (London: Michael Joseph, 1983), pp.

11-12, 19, 251.

6. Robert Gange, *Origins and Destiny* (Waco, Tex.: Word Books, 1986), p. 39.

7. Bernard Ramm, *The Christian View of Science and Scripture* (Grand Rapids, Mich.: Eerdmans, 1954), p. 148.

8. R.E.D. Clark, *Creation* (London: Tyndale Press, 1946), p. 20.

9. Pattle P. Pun, *Evolution: Nature and Scripture in Conflict?* (Grand Rapids, Mich.: Zondervan, 1982), p. 226.

10. Richard Lewontin, "Adaptation," *Scientific American*, 239, no. 3:212.

11. James Brooks, *Origins of Life* (Belleville, Mich.: Lion Publishing, 1985), pp. 109-10.

12. Robert Jastrow, *God and the Astronomers* (New York; London: Norton, 1978), pp. 12-14, 116.

13. William Lane Craig, *The Existence of God and the Beginning of the Universe* (San Bernardino, Calif.: Here's Life, 1979), pp. 59-60.

14. Jastrow, pp. 11, 14, 113-14.

15. C.S. Lewis, *Mere Christianity* (New York: Macmillan, 1943), pp. 3, 11, 15-19.

Chapter 3

1. John R.W. Stott, *Basic Christianity* (Downers Grove, Ill.: InterVarsity Press, 1964), p. 26.

2. C.S. Lewis, "Miracles," in Stott, *Basic Christianity*, p. 32.

3. Bernard Ramm, *Protestant Christian Evidences* (Chicago: Moody Press, 1953), p. 177.

4. Ibid.

Chapter 4

¹David Strauss, *The Life of Jesus for the People*, 2nd ed. (London, 1879), 1:412.

2. B.F. Westcott, *The Gospel of the Resurrection*, 4th ed. (London, 1879), pp. 4-6.

Chapter 5

1. Malcolm Muggeridge, *Jesus, the Man Who Lives* (New York: Harper and Row, 1975), p. 9.

2. J.D. Douglas, *New Bible Dictionary* (Downers Grove, Ill., InterVarsity Press, 1962) p. 1259.

3. B.B. Warfield, *The Inspiration and Authority of the Bible* (New York: Oxford University Press, 1927), pp. 299ff.

4. Gordon Clark, *Can I Trust My Bible?* (Chicago: Moody Press, 1963), pp.

15-16.

5. E.J. Carnell, *An Introduction to Christian Apologetics* (Grand Rapids, Mich.: Eerdmans, 1950), p. 208.

6. Andrew E. Hill and John H. Walton, *A Survey of the Old Testament* (Grand Rapids: Mich.: Zondervan, 1991), p. 437.

7. Clark, p. 27.

Chapter 6

1. Andrew E. Hill and John H. Walton, *A Survey of the Old Testament* (Grand Rapids: Mich.: Zondervan, 1991), p. 14.

2. R. Laird Harris, "How Reliable Is the Old Testament Text?" in Gordon Clark, *Can I Trust My Bible?* (Chicago: Moody Press, 1963), p. 124.

3. Ibid., pp. 129-30.

4. B.F. Westcott and F.J.A. Hort, eds, *New Testament in Original Greek*, vol. 2 (London, 1881), p. 2.

5. Lee Strobel, *The Case for Christ* (Grand Rapids, Mich.: Zondervan, 1998), interviewing Bruce Metzger, p. 63.

6. F.F. Bruce, *The New Testament Documents: Are They Reliable?* (Grand Rapids, Mich.: Eerdmans, 1959), p. 12-13. Contains a full discussion of the dat-ing of documents.

7. Bruce, p. 14.

8. F.F. Bruce, *The Books and the Parchments* (Westwood, N.J.: Fleming H. Revell, 1963), p. 178.

9. K.A. Kitchen, *The Bible and Its World* (Downers Grove, Ill.: InterVarsity Press, 1977), p. 131.

10. Bruce, p. 19.

11. Frederic Kenyon, "The Bible and Archaeology," in *New Testament Documents*, p. 20.

12. E.J. Young, "The Canon of the Old Testament," in *Revelation and the Bible*, ed. C.F. Henry (Grand Rapids, Mich.: Baker Book House, 1956), p. 156.

Chapter 7

1. W.F. Albright, "Archaeology and the Religion of Israel" in Howard F. Vos, *An Introduction to Bible Archaeology* (Chicago: Moody Press, n.d.), p. 121.

2. Millar Burrows, "What Mean These Stones?" in Vos, *An Introduction to Bible Archaeology*, pp. 91-92.

3. H. Darrell Lance, *The Old Testament and the Archaeologist* (Philadelphia: Fortress Press, 1981), p. 65.

4. Leighton Ford, *The Power of Story* (Colorado Springs, Colo.: NavPress,

1994), p. 13.

5. A.R. Millard, *The Bible* B.C. (Phillipsburg, N.J.: Presbyterian and Reformed Publishing, 1982), p. 9.

6. A. Rendle Short, *Modern Discovery and the Bible* (London: Inter-Varsity Christian Fellowship, 1949), p. 137.

7. Millard, *The Bible* B.C., p. 51.

8. A.R. Millard, *Treasures from Bible Times* (Belleville, Mich.: Lion Publishing, 1985), pp. 54-57.

9. Edwin M. Yamauchi, *The Stones and the Scriptures* (New York: Lippincott, 1972), p. 38.

10. Ibid., p. 39.

11. Millard, *Treasures from Bible Times*, pp. 47-48.

12. Yamauchi, p. 68.

13. Millard, *The Bible* B.C., p. 25.

14. Ibid., p. 27.

15. Short, p. 184.

16. Millard, *The Bible* B.C., p. 29.

17. F.F. Bruce, "Archaeological Confirmation of the New Testament" in *Revelation and the Bible*, ed. C.F. Henry (Grand Rapids, Mich.: Baker Book House, 1958), p. 320.

18. Ibid., p. 323.

19. Ibid., p. 324.

20. Ibid., p. 327.

21. Keith N. Schoville, *Biblical Archaeology in Focus* (Grand Rapids, Mich.: Baker Book House, 1978), p. 156.

Chapter 8

1. J.N. Hawthorne, *Questions of Science and Faith* (London: Tyndale Press, 1960), p. 55.

2. Bernard Ramm, *Protestant Christian Evidences* (Chicago: Moody Press, 1953), p. 140.

3. Ibid., pp. 140-41.

4. Ibid., pp. 142-43.

5. C.S. Lewis, "Miracles," in *Protestant Christian Evidences*, p. 143.

6. Ramm, p. 160.

7. Ibid., p. 40.

8. G.K. Chesterton, *The Quotable Chesterton* (Garden City, N.Y.: Image Books, 1987), p. 218.

Chapter 9

1. *U.S. News & World Report*, 1 December 1980, 62.

2. Quoted in *Christianity Today*, 8 October 1982, 38.

3. J.P. Moreland, *The Creation Hypothesis* (Downers Grove, Ill.: InterVarsity Press, 1994), p. 17.

4. Hugh Ross, *The Creator and the Cosmos* (Colorado Springs, Colo.: NavPress, 1993), p. 105.

5. Phillip Johnson, *Defeating Darwinism* (Downers Grove, Ill.: InterVarsity Press, 1997), pp. 68-69. Richard Dawkins, one of today's most influential biologists, states the evolutionist's creed of the "selfish gene."

6. Ross, p. 107. Here again Dawkins shows the atheist's presupposition that the existence of an infinite Designer is unthinkable.

7. Johnson, p. 76.

8. Moreland, p. 205.

9. Johnson, p. 77.

10. G.A. Kerkut, *The Implications of Evolution* (London: Pergamon Press, 1960), p. 20.

11. Kenneth S. Kantzer, "Guideposts for the Current Debate over Origins," *Christianity Today*, 8 October 1982, 23, 26.

12. A.E. Wilder-Smith, *The Natural Sciences Know Nothing of Evolution* (San Diego: Master Books, 1981), p. 131.

13. J.N. Hawthorne, *Questions of Science and Faith* (London: Tyndale Press, 1960), p. 4.

14. Johnson, p. 16.

15. Ross, pp. 19-20.

16. Moreland, p. 205.

17. Ross., p. 73.

18. Moreland, pp. 160-62.

19. Francis A. Schaeffer, *No Final Conflict* (Downers Grove, Ill.: InterVarsity Press, 1975), p. 16.

20. Davis A. Young, "An Ancient Earth Is Not a Problem: Evolutionary Man Is," *Christianity Today*, 8 October 1982, 42.

21. Kantzer, p. 26.

22.W.A. Criswell, *The Bible for Today's World* (Grand Rapids, Mich.: Zondervan, 1966), p. 30.

23. Kerkut, p. 3.

24. J.P. Moreland, *Seeds Resource Audio* (South Barrington, Ill.: Willow Creek Community Church, 1998).

Chapter 10

1. Hugh Evan Hopkins, "Mystery of Suffering" (Downers Grove, Ill.: InterVarsity Press, 1959) in J.S. Mill, *Nature and Utility of Religion: Two Essays*, ed. George Nakhnikian (Indianapolis, Ind.: Bobbs, 1958), p. 38.

2. Ibid., p. 13.

3. J.B. Phillips, *God Our Contemporary* (New York: Macmillan, 1960), pp. 88-89.

Chapter 11

1. *Open Doors, 1996–1997* (Annapolis Junction, Md.: Institute of International Education, 1997).

2. Ravi Zacharias, *Can Man Live Without God?* (Dallas: Word, 1994), pp. 126-31.

3. Bill Hybels and Mark Mittelberg, *Becoming a Contagious Christian* (Dallas: Zondervan, 1994), p. 151.

4. Ibid., p. 155.

5. William Lane Craig, *No Easy Answers* (Chicago: Moody Press, 1990), p. 102.

Chapter 12

1. Anthony Standen, *Science Is a Sacred Cow* (New York: E.P. Dutton, 1962), p. 25.

2. Orville S. Walters, *You Can Win Others* (Winona Lake, Ind.: Light and Life Press, 1950), n.p.

3. D. Martyn Lloyd-Jones, *Conversions: Psychological or Spiritual* (Downers Grove, Ill.: InterVarsity Press, 1959), p. 13.

4. J.B. Phillips, *God Our Contemporary* (New York: Macmillan, 1960), pp. 22-23.

5. Ravi Zacharias, *Can Man Live Without God?* (Dallas: Word, 1994), p. 141.

Study Questions

Chapter 1

1. What is your definition of faith? How does the author explain faith?

2. Why is it important to you to understand the truths by which you live?

3. How has your faith been colored by your previous experience?

4. Explain one of the ways God has shown all of us that absolute truth does exist.

5. Respond to the following statement: "Alleged intellectual problems are often a smoke screen, covering moral slippage."

6. Describe the role of doubt in the life of a thinking Christian.

7. How have people responded to you when you expressed a doubt about Christianity? How have you responded to others when they have expressed a doubt about Christianity?

8. Respond to the following statement: "Christianity cannot be just moderately important. It is either false and of no importance or true and of infinite importance."

9. Make a list of what you know to be true about Christianity. Include the reason why you know something to be true. Now make a list of your doubts and why you think you have them.

10. Choose one of your doubts. Make it a point to pray consistently about this doubt, asking God for wisdom. Also make it a point this week to look for resources that might help you (passages of Scripture, mature Christians, reference books, etc.).

> **God's love is more than you think.**

Chapter 2

1. The author quotes Mortimer Adler who said, "More consequences for thought and action follow the affirmation or denial of God than from answering any other basic question."

If you deny the existence of God, how does this affect your thoughts and actions? If you affirm the existence of God, how does this affect your thoughts and actions?

2. Why is it that we can't prove God by the scientific method?

3. How does Augustine's statement, "Our hearts are restless until they rest in thee" help to prove the existence of God?

4. How does the law of cause and effect help to prove the existence of God?

5. What do water and the human eye say about God?

6. Explain the following statement by Robert Jastrow: "For the scientist who has lived by his faith in the power of reason, the story ends like a bad dream. He has scaled the mountains of ignorance; he is about to conquer the highest peak; as he pulls himself over the final rock, he is greeted by a band of theologians who have been sitting there for centuries."

7. What does moral law have to do with proving the existence of God?

8. According to the author, what is the best and clearest answer as to how we can know there is a God?

9. Think of someone you know who believes in God. How has such a belief shaped this person's life?

10. Are you convinced that God exists? If you are convinced, what convinced you? If you are not convinced, what keeps you from believing? What would help you to believe?

> *Nothing produces nothing. If the concept of God is unthinkable, it makes sense for us to rethink our position.*

Chapter 3

1. Who do you say that Jesus is? How did you come to this view of Jesus?

2. According to John 5:18 and John 10:30, what did Jesus say about Himself?

3. How does the author respond to the question: Did Jesus lie?

4. What evidence indicates that Jesus was not a lunatic?

5. What is the legend theory and how has it been refuted?

6. List and describe the credentials Jesus used to back up His claim of deity.

7. Which of these credentials seems the most convincing to you? Why?

8. Which of these credentials do you struggle to believe? Why?

9. According to the author, what is Jesus' supreme credential to authenticate His claim to deity? Do you agree or disagree? Why?

10. Why does it matter what you think of Jesus?

> *Jesus Christ Himself is the Way to God. He is not merely a theological map to heaven.*

Chapter 4

1. Why is the resurrection of Jesus Christ the foundation stone of the Christian faith?

2. Why would Christianity be merely an interesting museum piece if Jesus had not risen from the dead?

3. How do the growth of the early church, the choice of Sunday as a holy day, and the words of the New Testament all point to the fact of Jesus' resurrection?

4. Explain the theory that the disciples stole Jesus' body from the tomb. What evidence discounts this theory?

5. How would you explain the theory that Jesus' body was moved? What evidence disproves this theory?

6. What do the wrong tomb theory and the swoon theory suggest about Jesus' resurrection? How have these theories been refuted?

7. How does the author explain that Jesus' appearances on earth were not merely hallucinations?

8. What did Mary and the disciples initially think of the Resurrection? How do their reactions help to support the truth of Jesus' resurrection?

9. Why did this one event turn a frightened, cowardly band of disciples into people of courage and conviction?

10. Do you believe that Jesus Christ rose from the dead, is alive today, and is ready to change your life, should you invite him to do so? If you do not yet believe this, what specific aspect of the Resurrection are you struggling to believe? Make it a matter of prayer and study this week.

> **We were created to communicate to a living and caring God . . . not to a stone idol.**

Chapter 5

1. Describe your experience with the Bible. Did you grow up reading it? What did those in your family think of the Bible? Has your view of the Bible changed over the years? How?

2. What does the Bible say about itself? What difference does this make?

3. When people say the Bible is inspired, what do they mean?

4. What do the writers of the Old and New Testaments have to say about the origin of the Bible?

5. What does Jesus say about the Bible? (See Luke 4:18-20 and John 10:35.)

6. Explain this statement: "Accepting the Bible as the Word of God is not the same as taking the entire Bible literally."

7. How does the term *inerrant* apply to the Bible?

8. Referring to the chart "Predictions Fulfilled in Jesus' Life," choose at least four of the events listed. Read the description of the event in the Old Testament, then read the description of the fulfilled prophecy. How does your reading help to convince you that the Bible is indeed God's Word?

9. The author writes, "As one reads [the Bible], the mind is enlightened, the heart is touched, and there comes a convincing discernment of the Scripture's message." How would you restate this sentence in your own words? Have you had this kind of experience?

If you have not yet read the four Gospels (Matthew, Mark, Luke, and John), choose one of them and begin to read a few verses each day. As you read, pray that God will speak to you through the words you read.

> *Reading the Bible with understanding is like eating peanuts; the more you eat, the more you want.*

Chapter 6

1. What do you think of the Bible?

2. Before Gutenberg printed the first Bible in Latin, how were the words of the Old Testament recorded? Why were public readings of these documents so important?

3. What was the earliest and most widely used complete copy of the entire Hebrew Old Testament?

4. How did the discovery of the Dead Sea Scrolls in 1947 help to prove the authenticity of the Bible?

5. The author states: "The New Testament was complete or substantially complete about A.D. 100." How does this completion date lend support for the authenticity of the Bible, especially as compared to other classical manuscripts?

6. What does the author mean when he talks about the canon of the Old Testament? How did it come to exist?

7. Describe the Apocrypha. Why is it not considered inspired Scripture?

8. What were the three criteria used to determine the canon of the New Testament? When was the decision made?

9. Read the following quotation and then restate it in your own words: "The Word of God is like a lion. You don't have to defend a lion. All you have to do is let the lion loose, and the lion will defend itself." How does the truth of this quotation apply to you?

10. Do you still have doubts about the reliability of Scripture? If so, write them down and resolve to do further study on this topic. Continue to pray for wisdom.

> **The words between the covers of the Bible are God's thoughts. Approach with care.**

Chapter 7

1. Use a dictionary to look up the meaning of *archaeology*.

2. Why are biblical scholars interested in archaeology?

3. The author states: ". . . we cannot prove the Bible by archaeology, nor do we believe the Bible on the basis of archaeological proof." What does the author mean?

4. Why were the discoveries of the cities Mari and Nuzi helpful to the biblical record?

5. What does the discovery of the tablets at Ebla tell us about the culture in which the Bible was produced?

6. What has archaeology taught us about Solomon?

7. Describe the archaeology of the New Testament.

8. Why was the 1931 discovery of the Chester Beatty Biblical Papyri so significant?

9. How do such things as stone inscriptions and coins help to verify the biblical record?

10. Respond to this statement by Keith N. Schoville: "Thus far, no historical statement in the Bible has proven false on the basis of evidence retrieved through archaeologic research."

> *Archaelogy impressively confirms God's meticulous preservation of His message for all mankind.*

Chapter 8

1. List some of the miracles in the Bible. Do you believe these miracles really happened? If you do not believe they happened, what keeps you from believing?

2. Explain the term *natural law*. What does the author mean when he writes: "It is important to note, however, that miracles are not in conflict with any natural law"?

3. What is the common definition of a miracle? What is the biblical definition of a miracle?

4. How do some people try to explain away biblical miracles?

5. What was the purpose of the miracles recorded in the Bible? Describe a biblical miracle that clearly illustrates this point.

6. How does the author answer the common question: "If God performed miracles then, why does He not do them now?"

7. List three reasons you can trust the reliability of the biblical recording of miracles.

8. Respond to the following statement by C.S. Lewis: "All the essentials of Hinduism would, I think, remain unimpaired if you subtracted the miraculous, and the same is almost true of Islam, but you cannot do that with Christianity. It is precisely the story of a great miracle."

9. G.K. Chesterton said: [A miracle] is power coming directly from God instead of indirectly through nature or human wills." Do you agree or disagree with this statement? Why?

10. Why does it matter what you think of the miracles recorded in the Bible?

> *Jesus Himself is the one convincing, permanent miracle.*

Chapter 9

1. How would you describe the conflict between science and Scripture?

2. Look up the term *scientific method* in a dictionary. According to the author, who developed this method?

3. The author writes: "The scientific method is valid only for those realities which are measurable in physical terms." Describe something that is real but cannot be measured in physical terms.

4. Describe the God-focused filter through which the Christian views science. How does this presupposition compare to the presupposition of the agnostic scientist?

5. Describe the three views of evolution. What do you think of each view?

6. How does the author respond to the commonly asked question: "Could God have made the world by using the evolutionary process?"

7. List and describe some of the recent developments in science that support Scripture.

8. What does the author say about dating the earth, based on the biblical record?

9. Over 100 years have passed since the French Academy of Science published a brochure that pointed out 51 scientific facts that controverted the Word of God. What do scientists think of that brochure now? Do you think scientists in 100 years will have a similar reaction to some of the current conflicts between the Bible and science? Why or why not?

10. The author writes, "We reiterate that the so-called conflicts of science and the Bible are often conflicts between interpretations of the facts and reality." Restate this sentence in your own words.

How do you handle the conflicts between the Bible and science?

> *The brilliant system of the sun, planets, and comets could only proceed from the counsel and domain of an intelligent, powerful Being.*

Chapter 10

1. Have you ever experienced a time of suffering? Describe your experience and your reactions.

2. According to the author, why doesn't God remove suffering and evil from the universe?

3. The author writes: "The ultimate answer to the problem of evil, at the personal level, is found in the sacrificial death of Jesus Christ." Explain this sentence in your own words.

4. What does the law of karma say about suffering? What does Christianity say about suffering as a punishment from God?

5. Explain how suffering can be related to God's judgment.

6. What part does Satan play in the suffering and evil in our world today?

7. Why are suffering and evil a necessary part of free will?

8. When you are suffering, why does it help to remember that God is the great sufferer? (See Hebrews 2:18.)

9. The author writes: "At times it is our reaction to suffering, rather than the suffering itself, that determines whether the experience is one of blessing or of blight. The same sun melts the butter and hardens the clay." Explain the meaning of these sentences by offering an illustration from your own life or from someone else's life.

10. Assume that you have a good friend who has just been diagnosed with a terminal illness. Your friend asks you, "Where is God? Why is this happening to me?" Write down what you would say to your friend. (Don't forget to refer to your own words when *you* encounter suffering.)

"Everything of value I've ever learned in life has been through suffering." **Malcolm Muggeridge**

Chapter 11

1. What do you know about world religions? Have you conversed with someone who follows one of these religions? If so, describe one of your conversations about religion.

2. What is the cornerstone of the Christian message? Why do Christians believe this?

3. What does the author mean when he writes, "To talk about the exclusiveness of Christ, a Christian is not assuming a superior posture in any way"?

4. Describe the *either/or principle* and give an illustration of it. How does this principle apply to believing in Jesus?

5. Describe the *both/and principle* and give an illustration of it. How does this principle affect belief in Jesus?

6. Why is the Golden Rule different in Christianity than it is in other religions?

7. Explain John 3:16 ("For God so loved the world that he gave his one and only Son, that whoever believes in him shall not perish but have eternal life.") in your own words. Do you believe this verse speaks truth, or are you skeptical? If you are skeptical, what specifically do you question?

8. How would you describe the three major world religions—Buddhism, Hinduism, and Islam? (Include their view of the afterlife and of God.)

9. What is the Jewish view of Jesus?

10. The author writes, "If we are to know the true and living God in personal experience, it will be through Jesus Christ." Have you had a personal experience with Jesus?

If it's the TRUE WAY, it is not narrow.

Chapter 12

1. Having now read this entire book, what do you think of Christianity? How has your opinion changed during your reading?

2. How do you react to the following statements?
   - "Christian experience is completely personal and subjective and has no objective, eternal, and universal validity."
   - "Belief in God is mere wish fulfillment."
   - "Christianity is for emotional cripples."
   - "Christian experience is sometimes positively harmful."

3. The author writes, "Christian truth does not rest on emotional highs." What does he mean? How do emotions figure into your view of Christianity?

4. Describe the role of the will in Christianity. (See also Ps. 34:8.)

5. When the author writes about the "personal inner confirmation" of those who have become Christians, what is he talking about? Have you experienced such a confirmation? If you have, describe it.

6. What are two questions believers can ask themselves to prove that faith in God is not merely something they have hypnotized themselves into believing (autohypnosis)?

7. The author writes: "Our personal subjective experience [of Christianity] is based on this objective historical fact." To what historical fact is he referring? Why is the fact so key to a solid faith in God?

8. Do you believe that you have been made for God and can find rest only in Him? Why or why not?

9. How does the Christian experience solve the guilt problem and the loneliness problem?

10. If you have already come to faith in God, what was it that helped you "go through the door"?
   Or, maybe you are like the young man in the author's living room, and you are stuck between the screen door and the real door. What will help

you go through the door? Are you ready to prayer the kind of prayer the young man prayed?

Dear Jesus,
I know that I need you in my life. I know that my sins are big and that I need to be forgiven. Please take over my life and guide me. Thank you.
Amen.

"Come to me, all you who are weary and burdened, and I will give you rest." Jesus Christ, Matt. 11:28

Books of the Bible

39 Old Testament Books

17 History Books

Genesis (Gen.)
Exodus (Ex.)
Leviticus (Lev.)
Numbers (Num.)
Deuteronomy (Deut.)
Joshua (Josh.)
Judges (Jud.)
Ruth
1 Samuel (1 Sam.)
2 Samuel (2 Sam.)
1 Kings
2 Kings
1 Chronicles (1 Chron.)
2 Chronicles (2 Chron.)
Ezra
Nehemiah (Neh.)
Esther (Es.)

5 Poetry Books

Job
Psalms (Ps.)
Proverbs (Prov.)
Ecclesiastes (Ecc.)
Song of Songs (Song)

17 Prophecy Books

Isaiah (Isa.)
Jeremiah (Jer.)
Lamentations (Lam.)
Ezekiel (Ezek.)
Daniel (Dan.)
Hosea
Joel
Amos
Obadiah (Obad.)
Jonah
Micah
Nahum
Habakkuk (Hab.)
Zephaniah (Zeph.)
Haggai (Hag.)
Zechariah (Zech.)
Malachi (Mal.)

27 New Testament Books

Historical

Matthew (Matt.)
Mark
Luke
John
Acts

Paul's Letters

Romans
1 Corinthians (1 Cor.)
2 Corinthians (2 Cor.)
Galatians (Gal.)
Ephesians (Eph.)
Philippians (Phil.)
1 Thessalonians (1 Thes.)
2 Thessalonians (2 Thes.)
1 Timothy (1 Tim.)
2 Timothy (2 Tim.)
Titus
Philemon (Phile.)

General Letters

Hebrews (Heb.)
James
1 Peter
2 Peter
1 John
2 John
3 John
Jude

Prophecy

Revelation (Rev.)